PRAYER: GOD'S TIME AND OURS

A gift from
Middlebury
Church of the Brethren

PRAYER: GOD'S TIME AND OURS

WARREN F. GROFF

BRETHREN PRESS

Elgin, Illinois

PRAYER: GOD'S TIME AND OURS

Brethren Press, 1451 Dundee Avenue, Elgin, IL 60120

Cover photograph by David Muench, H. Armstrong Roberts, Inc.

Cover design by Kathy Kline

Edited by Leslie R. Keylock

Library of Congress Cataloging in Publication Data

Groff, Warren F.
    Prayer: God's time and ours.

    1. Prayer. 2. Public worship. 3. Prayers.
I. Title.
BV215.G75 1984   248.3'2   84-19913
ISBN 0-87178-714-8

Printed in the United States of America

CONTENTS

PART THREE:
MEMORIES AND YEARNINGS
EMPOWERED BY CHRIST'S SPIRIT
Meditations and Prayers for Special Times and Seasons

1

PRAYER TIME

Prayer time is not measured by the clock. It is evaluated by its confessions, its intercedings, its grateful acknowledgments, and especially its empowerment by Christ's Spirit.

It is a time when we confess what we otherwise keep hidden even from ourselves—our deepest anxieties, our bafflement in face of the unexplained suffering of those we know and love and of our distant neighbors as well, our uncertainties about faith and the direction of our obedience.

It is a time when we intercede for others, not merely for ourselves. Jesus has pointed the way when he prayed, "Sanctify them in the truth; thy word is truth. As thou didst send me into the world, so I have sent them into the world. And for their sake I consecrate myself, that they also may be consecrated in truth" (John 17:17-19).

It is a time when we gratefully acknowledge "Grace as a Gift" (chapter 2). "Our time" has become *kairos,* or "filled time." "And the Word became flesh and dwelt among us . . . and from his fulness have we all received, grace upon grace" (John 1:14a, 16).

It is a time when, through the empowerment of Christ's Spirit, we sense that "Prayer Is a Fitting Response" (chapter 3) and that worship and work are alternating rhythms as close to one another as breathing out and breathing in. Worshiping is not simply a decorative piece tacked on like a bit of lace around the sleeves of a dress or a handkerchief peeking out of a coat pocket. It is the interior side of all we do. It is the way we gain perspective on our actions. By prayer everything is set within the larger frame of God's purpose as this has taken personal form in Jesus Christ. It is in his name that we are called, both to "Worshiping in Spirit and Truth" (chapter 4) and to the work whose shape is his own obedience.

The language of prayer is the language of the heart. It gathers to itself remembered phrases from the Scriptures, from hymns, and from other formative aspects of church and family. This, we trust, will be readily apparent throughout the volume and especially in the "Prayers On Selected Themes" (Part Two). What is remembered in our personal and corporate devotional and spiritual life we learned so long ago that we have forgotten when or how it was learned. But when appropriated and empowered by Christ's Spirit, all such living memories and present yearnings of the human spirit make prayer time both God's time and ours.

PART ONE

GOD'S GRACE AND OUR RESPONSE IN PRAYER AND WORSHIP

2

GOD'S GRACE AS A GIFT

Recall the current television commercial sponsored by the Smith-Barney Investment firm. The actor presenting this commercial is John Hauseman, well known for his starring role in the popular television series "Paperchase." Speaking with characteristic brevity and austerity, Hauseman applauds Smith-Barney's reputation and accomplishments. When he reaches his punch line in the commercial, his voice becomes even more somber, more vibrant, more compelling. He says, "Smith-Barney make money the old fashioned way: they earn it!"

Even as we hear these words, from somewhere deep within us we also hear a loud "Amen! That's how it should be." With a thousand promptings society keeps saying to us, "What you get is what you earn."

In sharp contrast the Scriptures say, "What you get is not what you earn, but what you receive is a gift."

But often, to our own loss and for reasons not easily identified, we hear society's achievement-oriented notes more distinctly than the grace notes of the Scriptures. We find it difficult to accept God's grace as a gift, freely given, gratefully accepted with "simple trust like theirs who heard beside the Syrian sea."

It is my hope that through this volume we will hear the Scriptures more accurately, more obediently, more joyfully, and especially that we will catch the grace notes. They ring so consistently from Genesis to Revelation and ring with special clarity and power in the Prologue to John's Gospel. "Grace As a Gift." That affirmation can be heard through several verses from John 1:1-18:

In the beginning was the Word, and the Word was with God, and the Word was God. He was in the beginning with God; all things were made though him, and without him was not anything made that was made. In him was life, and the life was the light of men. The light shines in the darkness, and the darkness has not overcome it (John 1:1-5).

He came to his own home, and his own people received him not. But to all who received him, who believed in his name, he gave power to become children of God; who were born, not of blood nor of the will of the flesh nor of the will of man, but of God (John 1:11-13).

And the Word became flesh and dwelt among us, full of grace and truth; we have beheld his glory, glory as of the only Son from the Father (John 1:14).

And from his fulness have we all received, grace upon grace (John 1:16).

No one has ever seen God; the only Son, who is in the bosom of the Father, he has made him known (John 1:18).

A noted Bible teacher once began a session this way: "If I understand what I am trying to do, it is to listen to what the Scriptures are saying and to tell you what I hear." In that spirit let me "tell you what I hear" from the verses just read.

God's gift of grace is not a mere afterthought. Grace springs from the innermost being, from the very mind and heart of God. For the gift is none other than the Word who shares God's own eternity. He is the very Word through whom all things were made, who became truly human and dwelt among us, and who makes God known with the fulness,the grace, and the intimacy of God's only Son.

God's gift of grace meets resistance. How foolish of us to turn aside from someone's gift genuinely offered. Yet we often do exactly that. The gift we reject may be from a devoted teacher who offers useful knowledge, enlarged sensitivities, and disciplined skills. It may be from a spouse who is eager to give and receive quality time for shared interests. It may be from a friend or colleague who cares enough to confront and to admonish us about some matter of concern. Or it may be from a preschooler who reaches toward with us with a drooping dandelion flower in hand, wanting only our attention and our agreement that it is indeed beautiful.

What folly to reject, to resist, or even to gloss over such gifts. Yet often we do so because of distractions, indifference, and self-imposed busyness.

At an even deeper level how foolish for us to resist God's grace as a gift. Yet again we confess that we do just that. When we are jolted from the sleep of sinful pride and sloth, when we are stopped in our

tracks and turned in new directions, then we see that in failing to respond we are among those of whom it is said, "He came to his own
home, and his own people received him not" (John 1:11).

But God's gift of grace is not overcome by the resistance it meets.
In failing to respond we let go of God, but God never lets go of us.
That is what makes it such a note of grace. In the movie version of
Boris Pasternak's novel *Doctor Zhivago* there is a deeply moving scene.
The Russian revolution is now ten years in the past. Major General
Zhivago has been searching for the lost daughter of his brother Yurri,
who by the time of his recent death had become a much-read and
warmly loved Russian poet. The search eventually leads to Tania, an
obscure laundry girl.

During repeated interviews the Major General keeps insisting
that she try to recall the dreadul events that happened years before on
the night she was lost. She remembers running with her mother and a
man, struggling to escape the violence of the revolution then raging.
The Major General senses she is close to tears and asks why her
memories are so painful. Finally, Tania blurts out, "Daddy let go of
my hand. He let go of my hand, and I was lost!"

The Major Gneral then says something like this: "Tania, that man
could not have been your father. It was likely Komarov, a family acquaintance of doubtful reputation. Your father was Yurri Zhivago,
my brother. Had he been with you, he would not have let go of your
hand. Believe that, and take comfort in it!"

If that be so, how much more comfort may we take in God's
steadfastness. In our folly we let go of God, but God never lets go of
us. That's the startling, freeing grace note of the Scriptures.

The darkness of our sinful resistance continues. We allow
ourselves to be deceived. We stubbornly persist in the path we have
chosen for ourselves. We stumble around as though the darkness
prevailed, but the light shines in the darkness and the darkness does
not overcome it. We cling to the darkness of sin that so easily besets
us, and the judgment we experience for our sinfulness is not only painful and real, but it also bears upon our eternal destiny in ways we do
not fully comprehend. And yet it is that very sin that has been placed
on the defensive by the still mightier power of grace.

Therefore, we sing of "grace that exceeds our sin and our guilt,"
of "grace that is greater than all our sin"; or we sing with Martin
Luther, "the Prince of darkness grim—we tremble not for him; his
rage we can endure, for lo his doom is sure; one little word shall fell
him" How can the principalities and powers of darkness long remain
standing? Though they still tower over us in their rage, when confronted by God's grace, by the light and life of the Word, they are so
shaky that one little breathe will bring them tumbling down.

God's gift of grace is full and overflowing. "And the Word became flesh and dwelt among us, full of grace and truth . . . and from his fulness have we all received, grace upon grace."

In one of its translations the phrase "grace upon grace" suggests accumulation and superabundance—"grace heaped on top of grace," grace that is at the same time "immortal love, forever full, forever flowing free, forever shared, forever whole, a never-ebbing sea."

God's gift of grace catches us by surprise, and that surprise is life-changing. "From his fulness have we all received, 'surprise upon surprise.'"

Anytime someone says "I love you" and means it, even with the mixture of feelings we all know in our daily relationships, it is received as grace, not as something we earn. It catches us by surprise. And it changes the way we experience ourselves and other persons and things around us.

To illustrate, let me draw upon a family incident that is described in a 1974 Brethren Press book titled, *Story Time: God's Story and Ours.*

Our son David in 1963 was beginning second grade. He had recently learned to write, really to print. When there was a household disagreement about such things as picking up toys, he often stomped into his bedroom and posted his feelings on notes stuck on the door, which he usually closed with a slam.

On this particular day he chose instead to send us an airmail letter, a piece of paper folded so that it glided through the hall into the living room where his parents sat. The letter was properly authorized by a hand-drawn stamp. This is what the letter said:

I'm not talking to you
Becuse YOU are rude!!!!
You helped some so why
not give in (see that) a hand with
picking up?
I feel like running away
But I LOVE You so I will
not.
I'm sorry I yelled at you!
And about the card game
you, do not have to play
it!
I hope you still love
me.
I forgive you xx.   air mail

Talk about a mixture of feelings tumbling over one another. Things are not right. Will they ever be right again? Disturbed, alone, ready to run away, uncertain, a little afraid, resisting parental authority, yet reaching for relationship, expressing love and forgiveness.

Talk about being caught by surprise, being compelled to see life from a changed perspective, and being constrained to live out of that changed perspective. I remember the incident as though it were yesterday. It was one of many events in family relationships that gradually required both Ruth and me *to be* and *to act*, not merely in the relationship of husband and wife, but *to be* and *to act* as parents of a sensitive, alert, sometimes rambunctious son.

Grace catches us by surprise, and that surprise is life changing. In very special ways that is true of God's gift of grace that issues in new life. It is based on a dramatically new status—that of children of God, born not of human will but of God.

As children of God by Jesus' own teachings and example we are taught to call God "Abba" and thus to participate in the intimacy of the Word, of the "only Son." With the full perfection only God manifests we expect of him the qualities of care and sustenance all parents fittingly give their children.

"Who of you, if your child asks for bread, will give a stone? Of if asked for a fish, will give a serpent? If you, then, who are evil, know how to give good gifts to your children, how much more will your Father who is in heaven give good things to those who ask?" (adapted from Matthew 7:9-11).

But this very God sent a beloved Son to confront the hostile darkness, to suffer the pain, the humiliation, the estrangement of the cross, to be "despised and rejected, to be a man of sorrows and acquainted with grief, to be stricken, smitten by God, and afflicted" (adapted from Isaiah 53:3-5).

Taught to respond to God as the heavenly One who knows how to give good things to those who ask, who, even more than earthly parents, never lets go of our hand—that my imagination can follow. I know the very direct claims that come to a parent and the urge to respond with care and firmness to a child's needs, even at sacrifice to oneself.

But taught to respond to God as the one who sends an only Son into a hostile world, a world sure to misunderstand the Son's mission, and to put the Son to death—that my imagination cannot follow.

Dwight L. Moody once said that he would walk five miles for a good sermon illustration and any of that quality deserved to be used more than once. The following—I am convinced—is just such an illustration. For the incident from the Martin Luther household that Roland Bainton describes in his book *Here I Stand* makes clear just how radically God's gift of grace challenges and reverses our expectations.

One time during evening devotions Martin Luther was reading to Katie the Genesis account of God's command to Abraham to sacrifice Isaac, the son born miraculously to Abraham and Sarah in their old age, apart from whom God's promise that they should be father and mother of the nations could not conceivably be kept. Martin drew a parallel between that account and God's sending his Son as a sacrifice so that we might receive the power to become children of God, born not of blood or the will of the flesh, but of God. Katie blurted out, "I don't believe it! God wouldn't do that to his own son!" Martin replied, "Oh, yes, Katie, that is precisely what God did!"*

"That is precisely what God did!" "For God so loved the world that he gave his only Son . . . " (John 3:16a).

"He was in the world, and the world was made through him, yet the world knew him not" (John 1:10).

But he remained obedient, obedient even unto death on the cross, carrying our alienation, crying in agony, "My God, My God, why hast thou forsaken me?" Yet "God has highly exalted him and bestowed on him the name which is above every name . . . " (Philippians 2:9). For "up from the grave he arose, with a mighty triumph o'er his foes. . . . "

"The light shines in the darkness, and the darkness has not overcome it" (John 1:5).

" . . . we have beheld his glory, glory as of the only Son from the Father" (John 1:14b).

"And from his fulness have we all received, grace upon grace" (John 1:16).

Grace like that can only be received as a gift! It cannot be earned.

Grace like that truly catches us by surprise! Only God could so love the world enough to place an only Son in the hands of angry sinners.

Grace like that calls for a grateful response! For "were the whole realm of nature mine, that were an offering far too small; Love so amazing, so divine, demands my soul, my life, my all."

Of those who hear that call of grace, let it not be said that "they earn it!" but that "they accept it!"—gratefully. For then they shall also bear witness, in deed and not merely in word, that they are those who receive him, who believe in his name, to whom—even now—he is giving power to be children of God.

*(Adapted from a quotation in "Heirs According to Promise," *Brethren Life and Thought*, Winter, 1980.

3

PRAYER AS A FITTING RESPONSE

In these changing times our Christian beliefs are put to the test in new ways. Some of the current difficulties we have in experiencing the meaningfulness of prayer follow from a long-standing tendency to think of God as a being "out there" or "up there" somewhere beyond the blue. We have been taught to speculate about what God is like: Does God know everything before it happens? Can God be everywhere at once? Can God do anything God chooses? If so, why is the world not a better place? Why do we have such a rough time following our own better instincts? Once we start down this road, God becomes a question to be answered, a problem to be solved.

We may come at it another way. When we speak of God, we are not talking about a being who is far off somewhere. God is as close as our own memories, our own relationships with others, our own projects, our own hopes and dreams. It is not so much that God poses a problem about heavenly things. Rather we speak of God as a way of asking a question that must always remain open, about what it means to be a human being.

Dostoevsky once said that if God goes, humanity goes. He is right. To acknowledge God, among other things, is to recognize that there are currents that flow in the depth of life that scarcely even ripple the surface. To ask the question of God is to ask this question about ourselves, "Who is this strange 'happening' on this planet earth—frail and strong, devious and noble, crying and laughing, loving and hating, sharing and withholding, always pursuing dreams that exceed its grasp, sometimes liking itself less than it ought, often preoccupied too much with itself?" To believe in God is to affirm that we have a nobler purpose for being than bone-grinding poverty, that we were not meant to grovel in bombed-out cities and defoliated countrysides, that we were not created for meaningless, routine jobs required to produce more and more things for a runaway economy, that we were not intended to endure lonely and isolated lives that follow from being forced to match the dehumanizing labels that box in the creative spirit.

And so worship continues to have a place. To worship is to receive the gift of responsiveness to those signals from the depth, those gentle—and sometimes not so gentle—nudges that keep us from capitulating to our cynicism, our myopia, our blinders. A whisper comes from outside us that we really are worth more than we think. There is a grandeur in the midst of all the sordidness of life. There is tenderness in the center of our manipulativeness. There is caring along with our callousness. Deceit has not totally overcome integrity. Sometimes trust breaks through the barriers of distrust. In worship we recapture a vision of that awesome mixture of life, of both the misery and grandeur of humankind. We scarcely know how, but in our isolation we sense that we are not really alone. It is as though another stands in our midst, and therefore we occasionally are free to reach out toward each other, to remove our masks, to forge ahead even when the path is unclear, to accept even those things about ourselves we deem most unacceptable.

Worship is a fitting response in face of the unexpected gifts and surprises of life. That is the reason celebration and joy often come to the fore. But the joy that worship brings is not escapist. It stands before our folly and our foibles, and the tears mingle with the laughter.

Then where does prayer fit in? To believe in God is one of the most deeply human acts we can imagine. It is a profoundly humanizing deed. It is to recognize something inexhaustible about the life each of us has been given. Like belief in God, prayer has its grounding in God's grace, but it is also our action. As such, it is a deeply personal expression. It is as human as crying and laughing, asking and hoping, cajoling and pouting, being sad and being glad. Prayer is a central form for that responsiveness that is so crucial in worship. We respond to those signals from the depth of life—sometimes in gratitude for what we have received (praise), sometimes in mute awkwardness as we find ourselves nearly crushed by burdens too heavy to carry (petition), sometimes in penitence for guilt we cannot shrug off (confession), sometimes out of concern for others around us (intercession). We speak and act out our feelings, our desires, our concerns, without knowing the outcome. Certainly we are not pushing buttons that somehow coerce things according to our own whims and private preferences. We face the securities and insecurities of life, trusting that we are sustained in ways we do not even know.

We are free, then, to address God with confidence that we are addressing more than a void or our own projected images. Jesus called God "Abba" and lived in a way that united the things of heaven and the things of earth. And now, since God is so profoundly "in" and "down here," we are even free to think of God as "out" and "up there." We need not feel constrained to answer all the speculative questions about what kind of being God is or whether prayer literally changes things. It is enough for us to believe and to pray as a response. We are not simply "deciders" and "dreamers." We are also "answerers." We answer those creative impulses that spring from the depth and that became incarnate in Jesus of Nazareth. That is what supports our belief in God and our confession that prayer is truly a fitting response.

—Adapted from an article in the *Messenger*, April 9, 1970.

4
ON WORSHIPING IN SPIRIT AND TRUTH

Jesus' conversation with the Samaritan woman at the well is told in John 4. The woman was surprised that Jesus, being a Jew, would ask her for a drink. She had difficulty in catching the true meaning of Jesus when he said, "Whoever drinks of the water that I give shall never thirst." By intuition she realized that Jesus was able to "read her soul," was even a prophet. She tried unsuccessfully to engage him in debate. The disciples were shocked to find Jesus talking to a woman, and a Samaritan at that. But the story concludes with the overflowing testimony of the woman that led many Samaritans to believe in Jesus.

This conversation portrays something very basic about Jesus as presented in John's Gospel. Jesus is the "way, the truth, and the life." He is the truth that drives out the menacing darkness and the truth by which we see all that is to be seen, for he is the light of the world.

Yet throughout the life and ministry of Jesus persons and groups repeatedly failed to "see" what should be so very plain! The Samaritan woman, the disciples, Nicodemus, and others found it difficult either to recognize who Jesus really is or to understand his message.

At a key point in the dialog the woman posed one of the standard items of controversy between Samaritans and Jews: "We worship on this mountain; and you say that in Jerusalem is the place where we ought to worship" (John 4:20).

Jesus refused to carry on the discussion in the terms set by the woman. "Neither on this mountain nor in Jerusalem will you worship . . . but the hour is coming, and now is, when the true worshipers will worship . . . in spirit and truth" (John 4:21b,23b).

With this conversation and John's Gospel guiding our thoughts, we may identify several important qualities of worship.

To worship is to give voice to those deepest inner yearnings of the human spirit—yearnings that cry out for appropriate expression. I think of a two-year old child standing on the front seat of a car while traveling on a hot day, a breeze coming in the open window, suddenly blurting out, "Thank you, God, for air!"

Worship issues in prayer expressions like that of the two-year-old child. Or like that involved in stating our fervent hopes in behalf of another as with a parent sitting up through the night, watching over a child whose fever is dangerously high, crying out, "Oh God, heal my child!"

Prayer may also take the form of penitence and confession—acknowledging our specific failings and our part in the estrangements and injustices that threaten us all: "O God, forgive me, and grant me the power to begin anew!"

Its form may perhaps be an urgent petition on behalf of oneself or maybe a spouse coping with a frightening diagnosis about the health of a marriage partner: "O God, give me strength so I can be available when I'm needed."

Or its form may be intercession for more distant neighbors in our country and in other parts of the world—neighbors facing the ravages of war, natural calamities, exploitation: "O God, quicken our compassion and our obedience so we can be instruments of your peace!"

Exclamations of praise in word and song, confessions, petitions, and intercessions are most appropriate in various times and places. Our corporate worship would be impoverished without them. But they are equally fitting when we are traveling in a car, by the bedside of someone desperately in need of healing, or wherever we find ourselves.

To worship is to see our personal and group histories from the larger perspective of God's dealings with all creation. Several summers ago I became more conscious of living out of a particular family history. I attended a Groff reunion at Groffdale Mennonite Church near Lancaster. I attended partly to discover whether my father was right on the meaning of the name, Groff. All during my youth my father insisted it meant "Count," "Duke," "Royalty." I discovered at the Lancaster Groff reunion that there was no conclusive evidence to support or negate that meaning. But I met many other Groffs who also clearly preferred my father's rendition.

I also gained a new sense of living out of a continuing history, out of a primary family story that helps shape our identity and sense of direction. A Jacob Groff emigrated from Holland in 1758 and settled in Rockhill Township, Bucks County, Pennsylvania. The last of his four children, Henry, was born on ship in 1758. He had earlier married Esther. One of their six children was named Abraham, born in 1800. Abraham married Deborah Shutt and they had a son named Jacob, born in 1836. Jacob married Anna Alderfer and one of their sons was named Elwood, born in 1870. He was my grandfather. He married Minerva Ruckstool. That is part of my continuing history.

Living out of a continuing history is also part of our experience in the church family. We work at nurturing a sense of belonging, at calling one another by name, at knowing ourselves in relation to those many persons who have preceded us. We enjoy shared memories. We laugh and cry together. We agree, but also often disagree, sometimes with charity toward one another and sometimes not.

In worship our personal and family histories and all these particular experiences in the church family are placed in the still larger frame of God's intentions and his dealings with all creation.

The conversation between Jesus and the the Samaritan woman refers to "salvation being from the Jews," a very particular, intimate group history. But we are called to recognize Jesus as God's Eternal Word, through whom all things were made, the One sent by God that through him the world—the whole world—might be saved.

God's dealings with the world are no less universal than they are particular. God knows each one of us by name. The very hairs of our head are numbered. Not even a sparrow falls without God's knowing.

Yet there is a "wideness to God's mercy, like the wideness of the sea." And to worship in spirit and truth is to see our personal and group histories from God's larger perspective—the God of Jesus Christ, the "God of the moving years, the God of the marching days," the God whose mighty "power made the mountains rise and spread the flowing seas abroad," the God who "so loved the world that he gave his only Son, . . . that the world might be saved through him."

To worship is to experience the faith relationship in firsthand, direct ways. It is to say with the Samaritans that "it is no longer because of the witness of someone else that we believe, for we have heard for ourselves and know that this is indeed the Savior of the world" (John 4:42).

In the church we number among our ancestors Abraham and Sarah, Isaac, Jacob, Moses, Aaron, Amos, Esther, Nehemiah, Elizabeth, Mary, Peter, Paul, James and John, and that great "cloud of witnesses" who make up the household of faith. Their prior struggles, failures, and achievements guide us on the way.

Throughout all gatherings of the church family we appropriately give careful attention to this heritage. We learn and draw strength from the testimonies of those who preceded us. But second-handedness in faith and witness is not enough.

We meet Jesus, yes, through the testimonies of others. But in worship the relationship becomes direct and deeply personal. We remember him with all the force of one who has walked with us, has talked with us, has broken bread with us as he did long ago with the disciples on the road to Emmaus.

It is as I remember my great-grandmother, Mary Ruckstool. She died before I was born. I have never seen a photograph of her, but I easily picture her in my imagination. I know her through the testimonies of others but also in a firsthand way. I remember her lack of formal education. But even more I remember her ability to stay steps ahead of anyone trying to get the best of her, her sparkling wit that kept breaking out in unexpected ways, her attraction to two-cent pipes that she discreetly used on occasion, her love of life and family, and her readiness to help anyone in need.

I speak with respect and love for Great-Grandmother Ruckstool and with full awareness of the clear differences between remembering her and remembering Jesus. But the analogy holds.

To worship is to be "stirred to build new worlds in Christ's name." It is to have our faith work itself out in active deeds of love and hope. It is to have our lives show in visible and outward ways that meeting Jesus makes a difference.

The Samaritan woman did not immediately recognize who Jesus really was, nor did she quickly understand his meanings. But she was changed in the relationship, so much so that many others came to Jesus through her testimony with a life-changing impact affecting their lives as well.

To meet Jesus is to undergo a radical, continuing conversion, to be "awakened" out of sleep, to be "set at odds" with our disobedience.

In worship we are made alive in a new existence that centers in Jesus Christ. "Whoever is in Christ is a new creature: the old has passed away; behold, the new has come" (2 Corinthians 5:17).

Our complacency in the church, our loss of clear vision, our settling for less than full and joyous discipleship, our lack of evangelical power, our fear of grappling with real issues, our lack of true growth: these are symptoms of the "old that has passed away."

There is no timidity in the way this witness comes to us from the Scriptures. The possibility of the new life into which we are summoned is as secure as God's promise that it shall be so. Our changed responses are as well grounded as Christ's triumph over the powers of darkness. Since God's grace is extended to us freely and without reservation, let our response in prayer and worship and in transformed lives also be fitting and bold.

PART TWO

LORD, TEACH US TO PRAY

Prayers on Selected Themes and for Special Days

5
ASSURANCE:
HAVING OUR MINDS STAYED ON GOD

Almighty God, we are grateful for life itself, for the many signs signs of your gracious favor, for evidences of health and vigor. Yet we confess our perplexity, our loneliness, our resentment and anger in face of the illness, suffering, and death we also see around us. An agonizing "Why?" wells up within us.

Lest we forget, remind us again, O God, that we can never be required to go where your steadfast love in Jesus Christ does not precede us.

Lest we sink and despair, renew within us, O God, the assurance that all things work together for good for those whose minds are stayed on you.

Through Christ our Lord. Amen.

6
CALL:
THE CALL OF CHRIST

Thank you, God for that deeply personal, that deeply disturbing, that deeply renewing call to service in your name, the call that led Abraham and Sarah to leave their home and journey to the "land of promise" in quest of a "city that has its foundations, whose builder and maker is God," the call that is heard most clearly in the life and ministry, the death and resurrection of Jesus Christ.

As we continue our worship and work, grant, O God, that we shall be newly centered in the sustaining, disciplining call of Christ. We would leave our self-centered preoccupations and journey to the "land of promise." We ask that the call of Christ intrude upon our inattentiveness and outmaneuver our puny defenses. Bestow upon us the power of renewed life and work that comes whenever we turn from the darkness toward the light of your eternal purpose Amen.

7
CELEBRATION

In Celebration of Student Achievements

O Lord, on this day of celebrated achievements we bring before you our memories and our anticipations.

We are grateful for the gentle—and even the not-so-gentle —nudges of your leading that have brought us to this hour: the restlessness that urged us on, even when our vocational goals seemed distant and hazy; the search for personal identity and meaning; the excitement of important tasks needing to be done in church and society; the example and sacrificial support of family and local congregations; the yearning for a center of faithfulness and hope that is more abiding than the ups and downs, the fluctuating moods of daily living.

We are glad to be here, especially when we recall how winding and slippery our paths became at times. We are glad to be here, caught as we are in an expanding web of relationships that seem even stronger as we contemplate the scattering that is soon to come.

We anticipate the new tasks and friendships that lie ahead. Without thinking less of all that has been accomplished and with continuing delight in the personal ties already secure we look forward to new assignments, new relationships, new invitations to ministry. We do not know what our tomorrows may bring. But we face the future unafraid because of your promise to keep us safe in the love, the faith, and the hope of Jesus Christ our Lord, in whose name we pray. Amen.

Taking Time to Appreciate

O God, we rejoice in special times of celebration with their closing events, their special banquets, and the moments when we take time to notice, to appreciate, and to state what we appreciate in fitting ways.

We are made glad by the ties that bind our hearts in shared tasks and commitments, by the years of study and fellowship, by friends willing to laugh when we laugh and cry when we cry, by the bread that strengthens our bodies and the bread of life that nurtures our souls.

So let this time be one of celebration, with gladsome table fellowship, nurturing memories, eager anticipations, and renewed dedication to the church and its ministries. Through Christ our Lord we pray. Amen.

8
CHRISTMAS

On Being Guided in the Way of Peace

O God, we are grateful for this promise-laden time of Christmas, for its memories and its anticipations, its food and its fellowship, its pageants and its melodies. Be pleased to grace this day with joyful gatherings of family and friends, uplifting music, heightened sensitivity to all those in need, and a renewed commitment to the One who truly guides our feet into the way of peace. Amen.

On the True Joy of Christmas

O God of Christmas, we are thankful for this special time of year, for its sights and sounds, for the music that fills the air and the heightened expectancy that rides on the wings of the angel chorus, "on earth peace among those with whom God is pleased."

Let it also be a time of joyful remembering and quickened anticipation. We would hear again the angel announcing "good news of a great joy that is to all people."

Let the joy of Christmas rekindle our affections and our actions, the joy that centers in Jesus, born in a stable, cradled in a manger, who for the joy set before him endured the cross. As we are strengthened by that joy, may the spirit of this season overflow in our grateful and obedient service. Amen.

The Christmas Spirit Rekindled in Our Hearts

Almighty God, who by the sending of your Son to be born in a lowly manger have kindled the Christmas spirit in our hearts, we praise you for all the delights of this season: for memories of your love and mercy beautifully evoked in word, song, and drama, for the enchantment of children whose youthful imaginations and overflowing enthusiasms reawaken the sense of wonder in all of us, for the delights of family and friends, for the privilege of receiving as well as giving gifts in the spirit of love and care.

Through these days of Advent let us be instructed and inspired, reminded and rekindled, arrested and aroused, so that our response may be worthy of your gracious goodness. May our deeds as well as our words give voice to that joy to the world whose firm foundation is the Messiah, the Christ of Christmas. Amen.

9
CHURCH

For the Church and its Worldwide Mission

We thank you, O God, for the church with its worldwide mis— sion. We are renewed in our faith and discipleship when friends in Christ join us from distant places. We are grateful for their testimony in our midst and for the ministry we share in the "one body, the one Lord, the one faith, the one hope of our calling, the one God and Father of us all."

Let our lives by graced anew by your living word. And grant that we shall be responsive to what we hear, so that we shall be strengthened within and freed to serve with gladness and hope. Amen.

On Behalf of Christ and the Church

O God, we pray in the strength of your faithfulness, for truly in your steadfastness there is no shadow of turning at all.

We do not ask that the challenges and tasks of our daily round will be removed, but only that the dimness of our souls will be taken away.

We share with you our celebrations and our concerns, those spoken and those uttered in the silence of our hearts.

We pray also for all those suffering the ravages of poverty, exploitation, and war. Bring peace and justice among the nations, beginning with each of us.

We thank you for the church with its global mission. Strengthened by your might and by Christ's living example, let us be found among those who place service ahead of status, love ahead of power, justice ahead of personal privilege, humility before you ahead of pride in front of others. May your renewal and blessing be upon all our relationships and tasks in behalf of Christ and the church in our nation and in all the other countries of the world. Amen.

Preparation and Consecration of Delegates

One: We gather as "partakers of the promise in Christ through the gospel."

People: Grant, O God, that our life together shall be gratefully centered in your steadfast love and strengthened in the "one hope of our calling."

One: We would leave our self-centered preoccupations and journey in the "land of promise."

People: We want to take our bearings from the One who is the "way, the truth, and the life."

One: We rejoice that Christ did not merely admonish us to seek the way.

People: He became the way.

One: His obedience precedes our own faltering steps.

People: Renew within us the willingness to have his Spirit direct our lives.

One: Keep us restless until we serve as Christ served.

People: Be to us a cleansing fire that burns away disobedience;

One: A mighty wind that drives away distrust;

People: An unshakable foundation that withstands the raging storms of doubt.

One: As delegates and participants at this conference make us bold in our response to your faithfulness.

People: Consecrate us for our tasks.

One: We are partakers of the heavenly food, the bread of life, Christ's broken body.

People: O God, strengthen our "feeble hands to shape a world for you."

Unison: Through our worship and work, our study and action, our fellowship and service this week, may the entire church be renewed in life and mission. Amen.

—For Church of the Brethren Annual Conference
Seattle, Washington
July 4, 1979

COURAGE

For Courage in the Strength of God's Promise

Almighty God, you have promised that wherever two or three have gathered in Christ's name, you are there in the midst. You have promised to make a people out of those who are "not a people," to put life into dry bones, to be to us a light that the darkness and night, even of death, can never overcome, to be a plumbline that never waivers in its measurements of truth, to be the source of life itself, in whom we live, move, and have our being.

Forgive us when we refuse to believe that we are "children of promise," when we shrink back from the sturdy claims of discipleship, when the call to obedience comes to us, when we are facing a blank wall. Renew within us the courage that enabled Jesus in his hour of trial to trust your promise, to face steadfastly toward Jerusalem, to say "not my will, but yours be done," to stand firm, even in that place of testing in which your will and Satan's wishes seemed confused, where the darkness of hatred, ill will, and death seems to hold its sway.

Renew within us the courage Jesus made possible by standing in our place, gaining the victory, and even now sitting at your right hand praying for us. In his name and power we offer our prayer. Amen.

The Path to True and Abiding Satisfactions

Thank you, God, for that life-continuing and life-changing call that comes from Jesus Christ:

—a call that comes from beyond all our imaginings;

—a call that sounds no less forcefully in times of sorrow than in times of joy, for it is heard both on wind-swept Golgotha and at a wedding feast in Cana.

As we continue our pilgrimage, shape our obedience in the direction of that Christ-centered call, for in it is the path that leads to true and abiding satisfactions in this life and the next. Amen.

11
DEATH

Comfort from Psalm 23

God, be to us a shepherd who leads us beside still waters, who restores our souls, who leads us in paths of righteousness for his name's sake.

God our Shepherd, walk with us through the valley of the shadow of death, so we need fear no evil because your rod and staff comfort us.

Surely then goodness and mercy shall follow us all the days of our lives, and we shall dwell in the house of the Lord forever. Amen.

Death as the Final Interruption

Death is the final interruption in our lives, O Lord. It brings with it loneliness, disruption, puzzlement, anger. Nothing in our human experience and nothing in our Christian faith allows us to pretend that it is not so. Death is more like an enemy than an easygoing friend.

But even in the face of death, O Lord, help us say with the Psalmist, "The earth is the Lord's and the fulness thereof, the world and those that dwell therein." "We shall receive blessing from the Lord, and vindication from the God of our salvation, for such is the generation of those who seek God, who seek the face of the God of Jacob."

Even when death seems to have gained the upper hand, O Lord, let us be assured that the gates have been lifted for us, the King of glory has come in, born in a manger, living an obedient life, riding a donkey through the very gates of Jerusalem, bearing our burdens. There is no place in which your mercy does not abound. For Jesus Christ has met death as the last and most formidable enemy, has gained the victory, and even now is seated at your right hand. Who is this King of glory? Jesus Christ, the crucified, risen Lord is his name. He is the King of glory. Amen.

For Those Suffering Bereavement

Thank you, O God, for that great "cloud of witnesses" who have preceded us on this Christian walk. We are grateful for their testimony, their strong example. Grant that we too shall be able to face the future with new courage, the courage whose foundations have already been established in Jesus Christ, the courage that helps us greet our tomorrows with trust in your mercy, even though the way ahead is dark and fearsome.

Thank you, O God, for making us members of the "body of Christ." In that body, that covenant family, we have our wholeness, we have our strength and our victory. For Christ has conquered every enemy of your will, even death itself. As members of that body we know a peace that passes all understanding, we know that morn shall tearless be.

Reassure us that we are members one of another, held firm by cords of compassion and ropes of love that nothing in all creation can ever tear apart. Through Christ, the head of the body and source of our life. Amen.

Healing in Remembering

Almighty God, we pause to remember. In remembering we sense there is healing as we open ourselves to your grace and truth. In the name and Spirit of your Son, who was himself no stranger to sorrow and grief, free us to remember pain as well as joy, to accept the tears that often mingle with life's laughter.

Day by day we are challenged to reckon with our own finitude and dying. In the face of death we are renewed in our gratitude for lively signals of human friendship, a firm handclasp, a hearty laugh, a twinkling eye, and an open spirit. We are grateful for the contributions other persons make to our life. Through their courage and dedication and by your grace may we be able to face the future with confidence, a confidence more firm than our efforts to grasp it, a confidence whose foreshadowings have already been given in Jesus Christ, a confidence that steadily moves us toward new assurances, new relationships, new acts of discipleship.

Continue to be to us a friend of friends whose concern is not more than a whisper away. Be to us a word of truth that is always true and always spoken in love. Be to us a counselor whose wisdom, empathy, and helpfulness know no end. Be to us a teacher who is the very truth that sets us free. Grant us renewed firmness in the calling we share in Jesus Christ, through whom we are bound to you and to one another with the full and lively certainty that nothing in all creation "will be able to separate us from the love of God in Christ Jesus our Lord." Amen.

In the Face of Death

O God, we confess that death brings a break in relationships and a loneliness that we find hard to understand and even harder to bear.

We confess our grief, our bewilderment, the heartache that tears away at our inner peace.

We are grateful that death also brings renewed gratitude for the gifts of life, the evidences of a warm, loving person, a quick "hello," an eagerness to serve, a courage in the face of failing strength, a gentleness of spirit, and a dedication to assigned tasks.

Help us claim your promise that death itself cannot separate us from your love, a love that leaps over every barrier. Give us the strength of Christ's own victorious resurrection so that by night and by day, at all times and in all seasons, we may without fear commit one another and those who are especially dear to us to your never failing love for this life and the life to come. Amen.

12
DISCIPLESHIP

Being Bold in our Obedience

O God, we praise you for the opportunities for fellowship and service that invite new levels of response. Translate our high aspirations into steady achievement, our worthy motivations into actions well done. Do not permit us to be mere dabblers and testers in relationships or in tasks. We wish to present ourselves before you as those who have no need to be ashamed. And so let us show forth boldness in our obedience, forcefulness in our witness, and humility in our service. Help us to remember always whose work it is we are called to do, and whose power it is that graces our own efforts beyond anything we merit or can even imagine. In the name and strength of Christ our Lord. Amen.

For Our Renewal and God's Blessing

Almighty God, we ask to be renewed in our obedience and to be favored with your blessing upon all our relationships and tasks undertaken in your name.

Give us your blessing so that we will be put in touch with life in all its mixtures, with life's poignant joy and life's joyful poignancy, with the tears that often follow close on the heels of laughter, with times of deep sorrow and the rejoicing that breaks out like thunder whenever we are able to trace the rainbow through the rain and lay claim to your promise.

Help us be as sensitive to the needs and aspirations of others as our own, so that we do not let life simply pass us by with the speed of a roaring freight train. Help us take time to notice, to appreciate, to give of ourselves to the persons and things of your good creation all around us. And help us take time to give and gratefully receive a helping hand.

Free us to spend less time and wasted energy denying our creatureliness, our finitude, and our eventual death, so that we do not have to draw back even from life's most scary parts because of our anxious care.

Our lives are measured in relation to the plumbline of your righteousness, and there can be no peace and wholeness until your own holiness and your own regard for the neighbor and fairness to all shape our lifestyle. So now and in all our tomorrows let us never forget that our work has no ultimate value unless our wills are aligned with your purpose as set forth in Jesus Christ. Give us a larger share of Christ's obedience, for it is in his name and Spirit that we pray. Amen.

Living in the Strength of Christ's Suffering Love

O God, whose love is always around us, we thank you for your overflowing love whose very name is Jesus Christ, a love that reaches toward our brother and sister with a basin and a towel rather than swords loud clashing, a love that suffers death on a cross on behalf of righteousness and peace, a love that sustains and will never let the righteous fall.

We confess our failure to love as Christ has loved us. We trust the sword more than the basin and towel as the way to get security.

So, O God, revive within us the willingness to live in the strength of Christ's suffering love. Keep us restless until our hearts find their rest in you. We offer our prayer in the name of Christ, the one through whom your love has been poured into our hearts through the Holy Spirit, the one who nurtures the life of faith within and sets us free to serve with the spontaneity of those who are your children, members of your own household. Amen.

The God of the Neighbor

O God, in whose power and wisdom and love there is fulness of life and perfect freedom, grant to us the love of neighbor that has depth, breadth, and height because it is not centered in the neighbor alone, but also in the God of the neighbor. Amen.

With Gratitude and Expectancy

One: O God, we gather in this place and in this hour with gratitude and expectancy.

All: We gather to be renewed in our obedience and to ask your blessing upon all our relationships and tasks.

One: Let the Spirit of the Lord be upon us, for we know that we labor in vain unless our wills are aligned with your purposes in Jesus Christ.

All: We gather to praise your name, to be attentive to your Word, to be admonished by our sisters and brothers for the strengthening of our faith.

One: Grant to us the power of renewed life and witness that comes when we turn from the darkness toward the light of your truth.

All: Overcome our forgetfulness and our stubborn resistance, so that we shall rise up like eagles . . . we shall walk and not be afraid.

One: Help us to look ahead with eyes clearly focused on Christ and ears attentive to his leading, so that we shall neither stumble nor fall.

All: We want to take our bearings from the One who was so united with your purpose that he rose victorious over every enemy, even death itself.

One: Let the thrust of our response be toward Christ's obedience as we begin another annual conference with its work, fellowship and service, study and action.

All: Then we shall know the wholeness and joy of those who have the Spirit of the Lord upon them to set the captives free. Amen.

—For the Church of the Brethren Annual Conference
Indianapolis, Indiana, June 20, 1978.

13

FRIENDSHIP

In Gratitude for Lasting Friendship

Thank you, O God, for the human ties that contribute so much to the meaningfulness and joy of life, for the friendship made strong and lasting through a shared ministry in Christ's name, for the certainty that time and distance can never unwind the bonds that unite us through the life and ministry of Jesus Christ.

Thank you for energies invested in common tasks, for the promise of relationships that grows still firmer with the changing circumstances of life. Remind us of the steadfastness of your love that surrounds our every breath. Thank you, O God, for all your gifts of mercy through Christ our Lord. Amen.

14
GUIDANCE
For Wisdom Greater Than Our Own

O God, let your Spirit of love and power and wisdom descend upon our hearts and minds. Center our discussions and actions in your eternal purpose. Overrule whenever we allow our own wills to go contrary to what you have made plain in Jesus Christ. Consecrate us for the tasks that have been given to us for the furtherance of the church and its worldwide ministry. We pray in the strength of your unfailing promise, the living guarantee of which is Jesus Christ, our Lord. Amen.

On Being Centered in God's Eternal Purpose

Grant to us, O God, a wisdom greater than our own. Give us insight illuminated by the light of your truth, courage tempered by your compassion, judiciousness made bold by your justice, which rolls down like waters, and righteousness as an ever-flowing stream.

We are grateful for supportive colleague relationships, for tasks that stretch every muscle. Today and in all our tomorrows strengthen each one of us by your might, so that in all our deliberations we may more perfectly think and act the way you want us to, for we pray in the confidence of your loving purpose, whose fulfillment is Jesus Christ our Lord. Amen.

For Christ's Spirit to Direct Our Lives

O God, we thank you for your immortal love that became flesh and dwelled among us in Jesus Christ. We thank you for Christ, who has broken down the dividing wall of hostility and made us one body through the cross, so that we are no longer strangers and sojourners but full members of the household of faith.

Forgive us when we continue to live as though your love were not ever full, ever free, ever poured into our hearts through Christ's living Spirit. Forgive us when self gets in the way of true concern for one another, when we want to dominate rather than serve, when we fail to seek first your kingdom of true righteousness and peace. Restore within us the willingness to have Christ's Spirit direct our lives. Keep us searching until we learn to be truly Christ-like in all our ways. Be to us a cleansing fire that burns away our disobedience, a mighty wind that drives away our pride, an unshakeable foundation that permits us to face the raging storms.

We offer our prayer in the name of Christ, the One who nurtures the life of faith and hope within and sets us free to walk where he walked with the true assertiveness of those who know they are held by a steadfast promise against which nothing in all creation can prevail. Amen.

On Being Receptive to God's Leading

Help us, O God, to be receptive to your leading, so that in all our comings and goings we shall see plainly in the light of your truth, we shall act boldly in the strength of Christ's strong example, we shall walk briskly and without fear, for truly your leading is a sure and steady light that the menacing darkness can never put out. Amen.

So That We Shall Neither Stumble Nor Fall

We are grateful that in Jesus Christ your light, O God, has shone so brightly that the darkness of sin and evil has not overcome it.

Forgive us when we crawl around in the dark as though darkness still prevailed.

Forgive us when we foolishly seek the dark corners of our own making more than the brightness of your face.

We make our confession in the strength of your mercy that is unfailing and of your goodness that knows no boundaries. We take refuge in your mercy and in your goodness, not as an excuse for our continued waywardness, but as the only source of our life and hope.

We are grateful, O God, for the gift of your Son, Jesus Christ, the One whose living example clearly points the way.

Grant to each of us the power of reinvigorated life and work that comes when we turn from darkness toward the light of Christ.

Help us to be salt that never loses its taste.

Help us to be a city set on a hill, a lamp set on a stand whose reflected brightness is there for all to see.

Overcome our wrong decisions, our stubborn waywardness, our self-deceptions.

In all our comings and goings we want to know the wholeness

and clarity that we receive whenever you guide our lives.

We lift before you our special concerns for those suffering bereavement of family and friends, for those with special needs, spoken and unspoken.

We pray for all, wherever they are and in whatever circumstance, especially for those who suffer from life's undeserved calamities and from the injustices we, in our blindness, help inflict on one another.

Keep before us the world in all its yearnings and unfulfilled hopes, the world for which Christ died.

Renew your Spirit, your compassion, your righteousness and your hope within us.

Restore to us the joy of our salvation. Be our guiding light so we will not hesitate or wander aimlessly, so we may perfectly love you and magnify your holy name through Christ our Lord. Amen.

15
HIGHER EDUCATION

Daily Renewal in Our Calling

O God of grace and mercy, whose grace is unfailing and whose mercy neither falters nor fails, we greet this new day with expectancy and a hopefulness that centers not in our own but in your strength and wisdom. We remember with gratitude those many dedicated servants who have helped form the communities of faith and learning we also seek to serve. We rejoice in the nurturing colleague relationships, the challenging tasks, the shared commitments that unite us as we seek to serve our institutions and agencies in behalf of the church and the world. We acknowledge the need for daily renewal in our calling. Strengthen us, O God, when the tasks seem almost overwhelming. Restore to us zest in our calling and in the carrying out of our ministries in higher education. Be our guide so that we may perfectly love you and magnify your holy name. Amen.

On Being Found by the Truth That Sets Us Free

O God, you who are the light of truth, whose light has confronted the darkness of human disobedience and darkness has not overcome it, whose light radiates most brightly from the life and ministry of Jesus Christ, we are grateful for the communities of faith and learning—homes, churches, colleges—through whom we have been admonished to love you with our minds as well as our hands and our hearts. Help us do so as our fitting response to the light of your truth, in which there is no dimness at all. Amen.

Responding Gratefully

It is by gifts of grace that we live and have our peace. We are thankful for the lasting friendships and challenging commitments with which the church's institutions of higher education provide us.

We are thankful for teachers who share their knowledge, their skills, their care, and their vision of the truth that sets us free.

We are thankful for benefactors who generously commit time and resources so that the church's educational programs can remain strong.

Bless us with the gift of gratitude so that we may respond gratefully to all your gifts of mercy through Christ our Lord. Amen.

16

MINISTRY

For Those Called to Serve the Present Age

O God we gather in the strength of your purpose because we know that all our work is unfulfilled and unfulfilling unless centered obediently in your eternal will. We are grateful for gifts far beyond our merit, for the call to ministry that simply will not let us go and that urges us ever onward to new levels of faith and obedience, for glimpses of that fellowship in Christ that is the one hope of our calling, for evidences of new life in our midst.

As those who are invited to pray for one another in Christ's name, we ask a special blessing upon all those who are called to serve the present age. Help them to be attentive to your Word, to the One whose obedience precedes our own stumbling efforts to find the way. By your continuing grace grant to them the power of renewed life and work that comes whenever we turn from darkness toward the light of your presence. Overcome their fretfulness and their anxiety, so that in their discipleship and their ministry they and those whom they serve may know the wholeness and freedom of those who have responded to the clear signals of your love and mercy. Keep each of them and us in your name. Keep us all from the evil one. Sanctify us in your truth. Your Word is truth. Amen.

In All the Days and Years Ahead

O God, you who will indeed rule through Christ, the Lord, you in whom we have all our allotted days, in these moments we are keenly aware of time passing, the farewells soon to come, the new relationships and new challenges soon to be faced. We have come aside one more time to say "thank you" for gifts far beyond our merit, for a call to ministry that simply will not let us go, for evidences of new life in our midst, for a robust grace that affirms and yet insists that we "go and sin no more."

We ask your special blessing upon each of those who are accepting a commission this day to a life of joyful and obedient service. For their unique gifts and dedication we praise your name. In all the days and years ahead grant that they will always be renewed in Christ's humility and love, in Christ's obedience and faith, in Christ's trust and hope. What we ask for others we also ask for ourselves. Strengthen us in our calling and in our commitment we pray, through Christ our Lord. Amen.

On Being Commissioned to Serve

Almighty God, commission us to serve, strengthened by a rekindled vision of Christ's church and the ministry we are called to share, a ministry whose commissioning is "to maintain the unity of the Spirit in the bond of peace," a ministry whose foundation is the "one body and one Spirit, . . . the one hope that belongs to our call, one Lord, one faith, one baptism, one God and Father of us all, who is above all and through all and in all."

Commission us to serve, renewed by the remembrance of that insistent call that centers in the obedience, the sacrifice, and the victory of Jesus Christ, a call that sets the "love of God and neighbor" in our very midst as the plumbline of our discipleship.

Commission us to serve, grateful for the larger church community, for all those persons who continue to respond to Christ's call, so that through their commitments our own faith is quickened. Through their commissioning and dedication may we be graced with renewed firmness in the calling we all share in Jesus Christ, in whose name we pray and in whose empowering Spirit we go forth to serve. Amen.

On Being Faithful and Fruitful Workers

O God, we are grateful for the relationships, the invitations to shared mission, and the opportunities for fellowship and service that await our obedient response. Translate our high aspirations into steady achievements, our worthy motivations into actions well done. Do not let us be merely tentative and standoffish in relationships or in the work of the church. Grant that we shall be able to present ourselves before you as faithful and fruitful workers who have "no need to be ashamed, rightly handling the word of truth." Grant that we shall have the courage and the wisdom to follow after Jesus, in whose path is perfect freedom. Amen.

On Experiencing Life from the Side of the Other

O God, grace us with true caring in all our communication. Help us experience life from the side of the other person, the other group. Help us be communicators who are also reconcilers, talkers who know how to listen, users of language who respect both the limits and the possibilities of the language we use.

Help us "speak the truth in love." Fill us with your Holy Spirit so we will be able to speak in other tongues, as the Spirit gives us utterance. Whether insiders or outsiders, whether religious or secular in our preferred language, grant that we shall be heard in our own tongues and in each other's tongues as we speak of your mighty works.

Hear us, O God, in whose great purpose our present calling has its charter and its goal, for we too want our quivering hands to be made sturdy as we seek to fashion a world for you. Amen.

Our Fitting Response

We go out from this upper room of God's presence. We go down from this holy hill.

We go and are restored in the conviction that God will be with us even in the storm and the rain, that God's presence is felt when tears fall like gentle drops and when laughter breaks out like thunder.

We go, strengthened by the continuing evidences of a covenant in Christ that our separations from one another cannot weaken.

We go and are made glad by anticipations of the new commitments and relationships that lie ahead.

We go, asking to be adventurous in our response, clear in our witness, and effective in the ministry to which we are called. Amen.

NEW BEGINNINGS

Attention to New Beginnings

New beginnings deserve special attention. Each such occasion points beyond itself to a newness that the world neither gives nor takes away, a newness that is more than mere difference and more even than the outcome of our very best efforts. Each new beginning witnesses to the newness that only God can give, that has already been established in Jesus Christ our Lord. And so let us rejoice in the newness that God alone can supply. Let us reach toward and live in the strength of God's promises. Let us serve and obey the Lord our God. Amen.

Facing the Challenging Days Ahead

O God, whose great mercies have surrounded all our yesterdays and brought us to this day, we are grateful for the successful completion of tasks undertaken, for times of relaxation and renewal, for the new relationships and challenges that stretch before us like an uncharted trail that is both frightening and fascinating.

We remember and ask your blessing on each one whose name we now uphold before you. Where there is anxiety, grant peace. Where there is loneliness, grant companionship. Where there is uncertainty about the morrows, be a light that penetrates even the darkest corners.

We remember and intercede for family, friends, and colleagues with special health needs. Be with all who cry out for restored vigor and wholeness of body and spirit.

We remember and pray for the worldwide church, for all persons and groups everywhere, especially for those who suffer from life's injustices needlessly imposed upon them, and for those who are poor and are always in danger of becoming poorer still.

Forgive us when self-concerns get in the way of true regard for the distant neighbor no less than the neighbor close at hand, when we seek to lord it over rather than serve others, when we fail to seek your kingdom of righteousness and peace first.

As we face the challenging days ahead, O God, we want to "own thy sway, to hear thy call, to test our lives by thine."

Grant us the ability to do so, so that we may be found faithful in our high calling. Amen.

God Who Makes All Things New, Yet Abideth Forever the Same

O God, you make all things new, yet you abide forever the same. During this time of new beginnings help us center all our strivings and hopes on your steadfast promises.

We are grateful for the tasks that are stretching even as they make us exercise. Help us move forward with trustful hearts, so that the expectancy of the moment may be translated into steady achievement in all the days that follow.

We lift before you our special concerns. Be close to each one of us with our particular needs: coping with anxiety in face of unfamiliar surroundings and challenges that threaten to exceed our abilities, coping with sorrow because of the illness and death of persons close to us, coping with struggles of faith and uncertainty about the nature of our calling. Be to us a strength and shield, a might tower that never shakes, even when the storms of life rage inside and outside us.

We pray not only for ourselves but for the church and the larger society, for persons in all lands in all circumstances. Remind us, O God, that there is no boundary edge to your mercy, that you are the Creator of all people, of all nations.

O God, you are the beginning and the end. You have set the stars in their places, and you have filled the earth with its fulness.

We see only a moment of time, but you behold the end from the beginning. Teach us again that you are the God of history who rules over every moment, including this one. We pray in the name of Christ, who began time anew. Amen.

On Beginning a New Year

Almighty God, we are grateful for the rhythms of life that allow us to begin again. We sleep and rise refreshed to greet a new day. We spend an hour in play and return to our work with new clarity and vigor. We serve others and find that our study has become more relevant. We absent ourselves from one another for travel and fellowship with friends and family, and return to the nurturing routine of our daily round. Grant that we will make the most of our new beginnings.

We are ashamed of the times we draw back because of fear and excessive self-concern. Too often past securities seem so much safer than your promise. We cling to old friends and shy away from the invitation to expand our circle of intimacy. We defend familiar ways of thinking and fail to give new thoughts a fair hearing.

Forgive our failure to greet new opportunities with confidence and trust.

We are also ashamed of times when we have been callous toward those things in our past that have brought us to these days. We become enamored with the new, and the old is too easily put on the shelf.

Forgive us when we turn too quickly from the past, and fail to learn from those who have preceded us in the pilgrimage of life and faith.

Help us to look ahead by letting us see where we have come from. Help us to look back but not to set up our camp. We want to take our marching orders from the One who so responded to your purposes that he rose victorious over every enemy, even death itself. Give us a larger portion of Christ's responsiveness and courage as we begin a new year of work and fellowship, of study and action. Amen.

On Facing the Future with Confidence

O God, we pause before you not to withdraw from our daily round but to regain our perspective in the midst of what we do. We pause not to retire from the race but to catch our breath and to pace ourselves for the hurdles that lie ahead. We pause not to forget our anxieties, our distrust and fear of one another, our unfulfilled aspirations, our broken dreams, but to remember these aright in the light of your healing grace and power. We pause not to seek a face-saving retreat from the hard challenges facing us but to ask your help that we may advance more deeply into the quality of discipleship that beckons as an open door because of the One who walked among us, died on a cross, and yet lives.

We would open our lives to your providential care so that we shall be more bold in our obedience, more humble in our love, and more courageous in our trust. Give us the ability to respond to the future that calls to us in Christ, the future that haunts and disturbs, contends and strives with us in the present. Include our tomorrows in your purpose by giving us the wisdom to discern what is truly in keeping with your will. Lift us above the petty and the merely private, above the cheap and the trivial. Ventilate the staleness of our self-centeredness with the fresh air of your kingdom tasks, of your intention for the world and all history as declared in Christ. Help us be your ministers, witnessing to the present and coming work of your hand, a work that promises to fashion a city that is built on rock rather than shifting sand. Make us servants of your purpose in the name and spirit of Jesus whose obedience issued in death on a cross. Amen.

Thankfulness for a New Day

We thank you, O God, for this new day.

It tells us of your faithfulness, which neither tires nor sleeps all the night through, yet is as fresh as the morning dew.

We confess our anxiety, our hesitation, our resistence, as we move toward the tasks and projects that lie ahead.

Sustain us all the day long so that when evening comes, we will be among those of whom it is said, "Well done, good and faithful servants. Enter into the joy of your master." Amen.

18

PEACE

God Has Promised

You have, O Lord, promised a peace that passes all understanding
    —a peace the world neither knows nor takes away
    —a peace made powerful in our midst by a babe in a manger, a basin and a towel, a cross, an empty tomb,
—a peace that frees us to work for justice in the face of the brokenness and alienation of our day.
That promise is the source of a call to active peacemaking,
    a call as new as each moment and yet
    as old as your eternal purpose for creation.
That promise is a plumbline that never varies in its measurement of truth, that assures us there will be no peace among individuals or nations until there is concern for the total well-being of all your creatures.
We shrink back from the rigors of that promise
    clinging to our fears and false securities, trusting our own strength and ingenuity more than your might and wisdom.
Yet we yearn for
    —a confidence that never lets us be complacent,
    —a confidence that lets us dream dreams of a brighter tomorrow without becoming idle daydreamers,
    —a confidence that impels us to beat bombers into plowshares and missiles into pruning hooks,
for such confidence has its source in your own reliable promise keeping. You keep your promises, and Jesus Christ is the guarantee that it is so!

In the strength of that gracious initiative on our behalf grant that we will be active peacemakers. We would be empowered by the Spirit of Christ
—to leave our self-centered timidities and puny defenses,
—to journey in the "land of promise," to help fashion that world community whose "builder and maker is God,"
—to walk the way of the One we nailed upon the tree,
for then all creation is alive with promise, its claim to confidence as certain as the truth that sets us free.
Printed as a "Congregational Meditation" by Church of the Brethren General Board, 1451 Dundee Avenue Elgin, Illinois 60120, August 1978.

The Peace of God Go With You

Go in gratitude, for God is gracious.
Go in freedom, for God has set you free.
Go in confidence, for God lives and reigns.
Go in hope, for God is establishing a new heaven and a new earth in our midst.
Go, and the peace of God go with you. Amen.

Peacemakers in Behalf of Planet Earth

O God, in whose great purpose an age is but a day, you who watch sun give up place to sun and planets burn away, forgive us when we forget the scope of your purpose, when like frightened children we want to be treated like the only objects of your love. Forgive us when we raise our fists in anger against other groups, other nations, other worlds that also belong within the circle of your care and sovereign power. Forgive us when we violate the natural environment so graciously given to sustain us in life, when we contaminate the rivers, the air, the earth, and forget that these too are full partners with us in your creation.

Be especially close to those this day who are facing very urgent needs, those whose lives have been disrupted and who have been made anxious because of the threat of a nuclear catastrophe, those with special health concerns related to the contamination of our environment, those seeking to apply their knowledge and skill to care for your earth.

Forgive us when our lifestyles contribute to the constant escalation of energy demands and the exploitation of the earth's resources. Restore within us the trust that enables us to be active peacemakers in behalf of this planet earth, for this too, we humbly confess, is upheld by your sovereign power and loving care. Amen.

19
PENITENCE

For the Grace of Penitence

O God, you who have disclosed the light of your glory in the face of Jesus Christ, you who have revealed yourself as merciful in your might and mighty in your mercy, you who have taught us that in returning and rest there is strength, help us to become who we are meant to be in Jesus Christ, new creatures and heirs of Christ's own righteousness. Grant that we shall grow in grace and Christ-likeness. Help us put aside the old and put on the new. Having been buried with Christ in baptism, grant that our lives shall show forth the true resurrection spirit.

We repent of our self-satisfaction, our contentment, our indifference that permit walls to stand and shut the other person out.

Forgive us when we attempt so feverishly to build personal relationships that we forget where our true freedom for the neighbor is to be found.

We repent of the times we take our discipleship for granted and fail to devote ourselves to our high calling with imagination, purpose, and resourcefulness.

Forgive us for the times when excessive anxiety and lack of trust deprive us of the joy of the calling that is ours as disciples of Christ Jesus.

We repent of the tendency to look upon the other person as clay to fashion in our own image rather than as your child destined to grow into the fulness of the stature of Christ.

Forgive us for those moments when we fail to see ourselves as followers of Christ, whose response was undergirded by his prior obedience.

We repent for shrinking back from the difficult tasks that threaten and challenge us.

Forgive us when we bury rather than use our talents as grateful and responsible stewards.

We repent of our tendency to cling to past values, methods, conceptions of the church and its ministry.

Forgive us when, in the interest of novelty and change, we

dismiss too easily the treasures of the past.

Lord, we repent.

Forgive us our smugness, our complacency, our inability to repent.

Lord, we are penitent.

Forgive us for our impenitence.

Lord, we are grateful for your grace.

Forgive us for our ingratitude.

Lord, we believe.

Forgive us for our unbelief.

Lord, we bow before you in prayer . . . but teach us how to pray.

Our Father who art in heaven, hallowed be thy name. Thy kingdom come. Thy will be done on earth, as it is in heaven. Give us this day our daily bread. Forgive us our debts as we forgive our debtors. And lead us not into temptation, but deliver us from evil. For thine is the kingdom, and the power, and the glory, for ever. Amen.

20

PRAISE

Sing Unto the Lord

O God, you who are the source of life and truth and grace, we ask to be empowered anew for service in Christ's name. Pour out your Spirit from above, and give life to all our fallen spirits so that we may bear witness to your faithfulness in word and deed.

Renew within us the eagerness to live in the strength of Christ's example.

Rekindle your flame of truth in the midst of all our restless searching.

Refashion us in your image even when we proudly try to live life on our own terms.

Bless all those suffering a restriction of freedom, those whose efforts to be faithful meet open hostility, those who are ravaged by the economic exploitation of the weak by the strong.

Minister also to those persons known to us by name, those in urgent need of healing and restored wholeness, those family members required to stand by when someone they love faces serious illness, those coping with broken relationships and burdens almost too heavy to bear.

O God, may we all be strengthened with might through your Spirit so we will be able to serve and sing to you, to make a joyful noise to the Rock of our salvation. Amen.

God as Alpha and Omega

Almighty God, we rejoice that Christ, the One directly conceived by your love, walked among us to guide our faltering steps in his direction. Renew in us the willingness to have his Spirit direct our lives. Keep us restless until we find ways to serve as Christ served. Be to us a raging fire that burns away the chaff of our rebellion, a cleansing wind that drives away the dust that obscures our vision, a reinforced pillar of righteousness that shores up our sagging discipleship. Be to us the Alpha and Omega, the source and the sustenance, before whom all persons, all powers, all dominions bow in praise and Christlike service. Amen.

21
TABLE GRACES

Breaking Bread in Thoughtfulness

For the bread that nourishes the body, and especially for the bread of life that sustains the soul, we give you thanks, O God.

As we break bread together at this table we remember Jesus Christ, whose body was broken for us so that we too might live in the power of his resurrection. Help us to live that way today and every day. Amen.

Seeking First God's Kingdom

We praise you, O Lord, for food and fellowship and for the sustenance and strength these blessings of life provide.

We freely and gratefully acknowledge that all such gifts come from your hand.

Keep us from being excessively self-congratulatory or self-depreciating, from succumbing to the pride that makes us pompous and the guilt that makes us grovel in despair, as we note the many things that add to our comfort and well-being.

Keep us aware that neither "those who have" nor "those who have not" always receive "only what they deserve," so that we may respond with the humility that is also made perfect in deeds of active love and in deepened determination to follow after Jesus, through whose obedience we too may first seek your kingdom and your righteousness. Amen.

22

THANKSGIVING

In Thankful Living

On this special day of Thanksgiving we affirm that your promise in Jesus Christ is more certain than the rising and setting of the sun, more reliable than the rotation of the earth on its axis, more predictable even than the changing of the seasons; for you are the all-sovereign Creator of the heavens and the earth, and your promise is true, for Jesus Christ is your own living signature guaranteeing that it is so.

We shrink back from the uncertainties we willfully associate with your promise, we cling to our fear and timidity like a security blanket, but we yearn for a confidence that is free even as it frees us to begin anew. Thank you, God, for a confidence that is as steadfast as your covenant promise.

We have felt despair, uncertainty, and an agonizing sense of distance between our aspirations and our achievements, but we have also seen the early dawning of a faithfulness more firm than our own efforts to achieve it, a faithfulness whose foreshadowings have already been given in Jesus Christ, a faithfulness that challenges both smug complacency and nervous attempts at self-justification. Thank you, God, for that faithfulness.

We have felt overwhelmed by the many different, often competing claims on our life energies, but we also hear whispers of a uniting purpose that the world neither gives nor takes away, a purpose that enables us to "mount up with wings as eagles, to run and not be weary, to walk and not faint." Thank you, God, for that purpose.

We are at times burdened by anxious cares, by struggles of health, by strained relationships, by needs that stretch every nerve and make us doubt whether we can go on. Grant to us and to others for whom we pray a renewed experience of your healing power and the peace that passes all understanding. Thank you, God, for that peace.

When we feel left out, when the circle seems closed to us, we speak with the hopefulness of those who are known and loved by Jesus Christ, the one who never forgets our name. Thank you, God, for an identity that is at once a gift and a promise-filled task. Amen.

23

WORLD

The World That God Loved So Much

O God, by whose strength even those of us who are weak are made strong, we pray in the certitude made possible by your might and your steadfastness; we pray in the full and blessed assurance of your unshakable trustworthiness.

We offer to you our special concerns. For those suffering bereavement through the loss of family or friends we ask a renewal of that sustaining assurance that nothing in all creation can ever separate us from your love made personal and powerful in Jesus Christ. We pray for distant neighbors as well as those close at hand. Comfort all persons with special needs, all who suffer from injustice and life's calamities. Keep before us concern for your world, yes, for that very world so centered in your love that you sent your only Son to suffer and die in its behalf.

Renewed in gratitude and in the joy of our calling, lift us, O God, to new levels of service and evangelical witness so that "the world might believe." Amen.

PART THREE

MEMORIES AND YEARNINGS
EMPOWERED BY CHRIST'S SPIRIT

Meditations and Prayers for Special Times and Seasons

24
ANOINTING

Cleansed and Commissioned by His Obedience

Have this mind among yourselves, which you have in Christ Jesus, who, though he was in the form of God, did not count equality with God a thing to be grasped, but emptied himself, taking the form of a servant, being born in our likeness. And being found in human form he humbled himself and became obedient unto death, even death on a cross" (Philippians 2:5-8).

This Scripture passage offers a picture of Jesus facing and resisting temptation.

The question is whether preoccupation with the prerogatives of his unique relationship with God will divert him from his mission in behalf of men and women who are locked in the grip of sin, death, law, and the devil. That mission involves an almost unimaginable contrast between his heavenly and earthly natures, of being "in the form of God" and being in the "form of a slave."

The text is clear about the outcome, even as it acknowledges the option Jesus faced. "He did not count equality with God a thing to be grasped."

"A thing to be grasped" evokes the image of a prize to be grabbed. Its vividness and earthiness as an image requires us to think not only of a heavenly struggle but also of Jesus' earthly mission as God's anointed. Recall how Jesus in the wilderness was tempted by a dazzling display of power to lay claim to this divine glory that, as the devil would have him believe, was really his to call upon (Luke 4:5-12).

By thus using inappropriate worldly means to raise himself to a political Messiahship, Jesus would then have chosen to lord it over rather than serve the kingdoms of the world. "Being in the form of God" would then have been something to be grabbed, something held close and used as a security hedge against the mission actually chosen, i.e., the long, bitter, sorrowful way of humiliation, suffering, and death.

But Jesus "emptied himself." He gave up all special prerogatives based on divine origin and status. He gave up all claim to the privileges and powers of divine glory. He became the true penitent, confessing for us and in our place that God alone has the right to rule. Himself without sin, "he was made to be sin so that we might become the righteousness of God."

Jesus took the "form of a servant," fulfilling the prophecy of Isaiah 52:13 of a servant who, while obedient, would suffer and die and finally be exalted.

"He humbled himself and became obedient unto death, even death on a cross." The stress is on the obedience of Jesus. "Unto death" is the qualifier that reminds us of the depth of Jesus' obedience. Death on a cross meant that Jesus suffered the fate of a slave, the deepest form of shame. Death on a cross implied for a Jew not merely loss of citizenship but even total loss of the divine presence.

Jesus as the true penitent stood in the place of persons held fast by sin, death, law, and the devil. Even in that place of awful contradiction he did not grab at "equality with God" but endured the humiliation, the fullest contradiction to the honor and glory that belonged to him in the "form of God."

"Unto death" points toward the Passion as the culmination of Jesus' mission and underscores the radical character of his obedience. But the significance of his death is related to the actual content of his life and ministry. That content is clearly presupposed in the way Philippians draws discipleship implications from "having this mind among ourselves, that we have in Christ Jesus." "Do nothing from selfishness or conceit, but in humility count others better than yourself. Let each of you look not only to your own interests, but also to the interests of others" (Philippians 2:3-4).

Triumphal Entry

The clash between Jesus' chosen path as God's anointed and popular expectations is clear if we recall Jesus' interchange with his disciples immediately prior—actually on the way—to Jerusalem for what we know as the "Triumphal Entry" (Matthew 20 and 21).

Jesus took his disciples aside and said, "The Son of man will be delivered to the chief priests and scribes, and they will condemn him to death, and deliver him to the Gentiles to be mocked and scourged and crucified, and he will be raised on the third day" (Matthew 20:18,19).

Hearing but not comprehending, the mother of the sons of Zebedee immediately had a favor to ask. "Command that these two sons of mine may sit, one at your right hand and one at your left, in your kingdom" (Matthew 20:21).

Jesus said, "Do you know what you are asking?" Then he turned to the two sons: "Are you able to drink the cup that I am to drink?" They said: "We are able." Jesus said, "You will drink my cup, but to sit at my right hand and my left is not mine to grant, but it is for those for whom it has been prepared by my Father" (Matthew 20:22-23).

When the other ten disciples heard it, they were indignant, probably out of chagrin that they might be upstaged on who would have the privileged positions.

Jesus then said to them all, "You know that the rulers of the Gentiles lord it over them, and their great men exercise authority over them. It shall not be so among you; but whoever would be great among you must be your slave; even as the Son of man came not to be served but to serve, and to give his life as a ransom for many" (Matthew 20:25,26).

As they traveled toward Jerusalem, two blind men cried out, "Have mercy on us, Son of David!" The crowd tried to keep them quiet, but the men shouted all the more, "Lord, have mercy on us, Son of David!" Jesus touched their eyes and their sight returned. Sightless, these men saw more than did the disciples and the crowd who were gifted with physical sight. They saw that Jesus' mission was to heal and to serve.

As they approached Bethphage at the Mount of Olives, Jesus sent two disciples to the village to find a donkey and colt. He assured them that all had been prepared. They were simply to appropriate the animals and bring them to him. If stopped, they were to say, "The Lord has need of them."

Matthew's account sees all this as fulfilling Zechariah's prophecy, "Behold, your King is coming to you, humble, and mounted on an ass, and on a colt, the foal of an ass" (Matthew 21:5,6).

The procession began. The crowd spread their garments on the road, much as the followers of the Old Testament King Jehu placed garments on the stairs when he was proclaimed king (2 Kings 9:13).

The crowd cut branches—myrtle, willow, palm leaf—and made a

carpet to mark off the demonstration route. They shouted, "Hosanna," meaning, "Save Now! Help us, we pray! Help Israel, God!" thus echoing the blind men's shout.

But the crowd, like the mother of the sons of Zebedee and the disciples, added specific political overtones as they went on to say, "Hosanna to the Son of David! Blessed is he who comes in the name of the Lord."

Jesus' entry into Jerusalem resulted in what amounted to a messianic demonstration. Jesus' own chosen path, "taking the form of a servant," clashed with a variety of popular expectations. His mission centered among Jews who had been oppressed for hundreds of years. Whenever they seemed to be getting ahead as a nation, some larger empire—Assyria, Babylonia, Persia, Egypt—would overrun and enslave them. They were looking for a vindicator, a deliverer who would deserve the title "Messiah" (the anointed one), a Messiah who would set them free and through whom God's reign would be established on earth.

What would that Messiah be like? A descendant of David who would rule the way King David did, who would reestablish the Davidic blessings of land, food, and prestige as well as peace and justice? A warrior Messiah, whether from the house of David or not, who would push the Romans back into the sea and free the land from foreign oppression? A heavenly creature, sent down from the clouds of heaven, with legions of angels, who would break the Roman yoke and set up his heavenly kingdom in Palestine?

Jesus' messianic demonstration said forcefully that he came in gentleness, riding on a donkey, a beast of burden. In the prophetic tradition with which Jesus is identified, the donkey symbolized humility, service, peace. Welcomed by many as a man of war, he came as a man of peace. Welcomed as one who would wield military might for the enhancement of a particular nation, he came exemplifying the power of love in behalf of all nations. Welcomed by those who often put status ahead of service, he came "not to be served but to serve, and to give his life as a ransom for many."

The Feet Washing

The feet washing scene of John 13 is one of the very familiar passages for all of us. This presents another vivid picture of Jesus being in the "form of a servant," literally, a slave.

It was the slave's duty, while guests reclined at the table before the meal began, to come behind the couch and wash their feet. In an unprecedented way, Jesus, the host at the supper, performed this menial service. He rose from supper, laid aside his garments, girded himself with a towel, and poured water into the basin in preparation for washing the feet of the disciples.

Peter voiced the disbelief of the others, "Lord, what are you doing? You will never wash my feet."

Jesus answered, "If I do not wash you, you have no part in me."

Then with his characteristic impulsiveness Peter wanted his hands and his head washed as well, just to be sure that he was properly cleansed.

Jesus reassured Peter, "He who has bathed does not need to wash, except for his feet, but he is clean all over."

And then, to the continuing surprise of all those present, Jesus, taking the "form of a servant," humbled himself, performing the most menial work of a slave, eventually dying on a cross, the depth of humiliation, the ultimate contrast for one who is in "the form of God."

This supper meal with the disciples just prior to his death on a cross was a time for consolidating teachings and deepening the bonds of fellowship in anticipation of what was soon to come.

The need for cleansing to which Jesus refers in the act of feet washing is very apparent. Betrayal was in the midst of that intimate circle.

"You are clean, but not all of you. Truly, truly, I say to you, one of you will betray me."

The stirring among the disciples suggests their uncomfortableness. "Could it be one of us? It might be any one of us!"

The need for cleansing extends to all the disciples, even though the locus of the betrayal is in Judas. "The devil had already put it into the heart of Judas to betray him."

" 'It is he to whom I shall give this morsel when I have dipped it' . . . He gave it to Judas . . . . 'What you are going to do, do quickly' . . . . Judas left immediately, and it was night!" (John 13:26, 27, 30).

Jesus' Anointing at Bethany

We can get further understanding of the need for cleansing, this need that is applied generally to all the disciples but is focused in the betrayal by Judas, if we bring into view another familiar scene—Jesus' anointing at Bethany. On the way to Jerusalem Jesus had stopped at Bethany, the house of Lazarus, Martha, and Mary.

"There they made him a supper; Martha served, and Lazarus was one of those at the table with him. Mary took a pound of costly ointment of pure nard and anointed the feet of Jesus and wiped his feet with her hair; and the house was filled with the fragrance of the ointment" (John 12:1-3).

In John's account it is Judas who objects, "Why was this ointment not sold and the money given to the poor?"

In Matthew it was the disciples (Matthew 26:8), and in Mark it was simply "some people" (Mark 14:4) who spoke out with indignation at what seemed to be a wasteful act in the face of such great human need.

John characteristically presents Judas in a harsh light, charging here that he was really interested in keeping the money for himself.

All the accounts agree that Jesus reminded them that they have the poor with them always, but he would not always be with them, that Mary's anointing of Jesus is fitting in light of his imminent death and burial.

Judas' reservation is shared by the other disciples. Jesus' response to Peter—"If I do not wash you, you have no part in me"—confirms the point that uncleanness was not restricted to Judas. Rather, he represents the disciples' uncleanness and our own.

What was at the root of Judas' betrayal of Jesus, the betrayal in which the disciples and all of us participate?

There is no one answer! Interpretations of Judas vary: a pawn in God's hand executing a plan for our salvation, a misguided Zealot who hoped to force Jesus' hand in bringing the Kingdom even by violent means, an apocalyptic fanatic expecting God's miraculous deliverance as events unfolded, a thief and traitor without scruples.

There is an additional clue from the Bethany anointing. Mary responded with spontaneous devotion and gratitude to Jesus, the anointed of God, the One who took the "form of a slave" rather than clutch at divine glory. Judas, representing all of us as well as the disciples, withheld that single-minded devotion in the name of what seems so reasonable, namely the needs of the poor. But Judas' response is also an expression of the determination to set himself up as judge rather than to be open to God's anointed who allowed himself to be judged in our place, numbered among the transgressors, obedient even to death on a cross.

Upon seeing Mary anoint Jesus' feet, there were some (we could insert the disciples, Judas, all of us) who said to themselves indignantly, "Why was the ointment thus wasted? For this ointment might have been sold for more than three hundred denarii, and given to the poor." But Jesus said, "Let her alone; why do you trouble her? She has done a beautiful thing to me. For you always have the poor with you, and whenever you will, you can do good to them; but you will not always have me. She has done what she could; she has anointed my body beforehand for burying. And truly, I say to you, wherever the gospel is preached in the whole world, what she has done will be told in memory of her" (Mark 14:4-9).

Cleansed by his obedience. Cleansed by the objective fact of that obedience, cleansed from our own complicity in the betrayal of God's anointed, cleansed from our persisting tendency to miss the intrinsic connection between Mary's single-minded devotion and carrying on the mission of servanthood embodied in Jesus.

We are cleansed by his obedience. We are also commissioned by his cleansing!

Commissioned to extend his exchange in behalf of others. "All this is from God, who through Christ reconciled us to himself and gave us the ministry of reconciliation" (2 Corinthians 5:18).

In Jesus Christ, the one who thought "equality with God was not a thing to be grasped, but humbled himself, taking the form of a servant," God himself has experienced life from our side.

God met human betrayal at its worst. God encountered life's most formidable enemies—sin, death, law, the devil—where their power was the greatest. God sat where we sit, with our temptations and our sorrows, our victories and our joys, our anxieties and our confidences.

There simply is no place we shall ever be required to go where God is not ahead of us. "Where could I go to escape your spirit? Where could I flee your presence? If I climb the heavens, you are there. There, too, if I lie in Sheol . . . in the grave! If I flee to the point of sunrise, or westward across the sea, your hand would still be guiding me, your right hand holding me" (Psalm 139).

Since God in Jesus Christ has exchanged places with us, has experienced life from our side, we are empowered by Christ's Spirit to experience life from the other person's side, to extend his exchange in behalf of others, to carry on his ministry of reconciliation.

Commissioned to health. The service of anointing for healing presupposes the commissioning that comes by his cleansing—really the commissioning/recommissioning to health.

"Is any one among you suffering? Let him pray. Is any cheerful? Let him sing praise. Is any among you sick? Let him call for the elders of the church, and let them pray over him, anointing him with oil in the name of the Lord; and the prayer of faith will save the sick man, and the Lord will raise him up; and if he has committed sins, he will be forgiven. Therefore, confess your sins to one another, and pray for one another, that you may be healed" (James 5:13-16a).

This passage issues a call to simple obedience. The call itself is simple and direct. When one has special health needs, that one asks for representatives of the church to gather for prayer, confession, anointing, and the laying on of hands.

It is a time for the centering of our deepest hopes and expectations, our sorrows and joys, our fears and assurances, seeking release from those things that in any way separate us from one another and

God.

Neither the Scripture passage nor the practice of anointing places excessive weight on tidying up all our emotions and fundamental attitudes.

The call to simple obedience is a call to come penitently but also as we are. The accent is not on us but on the one who issues the call: on Jesus Christ, his life, death, resurrection: on his servanthood: on his unique status as the anointed of God.

It is a commissioning/recommissioning to health. Anointing and the laying on of hands within Israel and within the church as the new Israel point toward one person being commissioned by God, and the people being recommissioned in and with that one. The aim is covenant/wholeness/*shalom*/Christlikeness.

We are not required to romanticize the situation. Suffering, pain, and the death we all face seem utterly opposite to God's good intention for his creation.

Christ's prior anointing charts the way. He faced the suffering and loneliness that life inevitably brings, for he was a "person of sorrows and acquainted with grief." He entered into that frightening realm of suffering and alienation in which an alien power seems to hold sway, the very stronghold of sin, death, law, and the devil.

The scriptural call to simple obedience in the anointing service comes with the strength of Christ's prior servanthood in our behalf.

If we shrink back from suffering and pain, from restricted bodily and personal powers, so did Christ himself, who cried, "My God, my God, why have you forsaken me?" Our obedience is now undergirded by his obedience. "He steadfastly set his face toward Jerusalem." Taking the form of a servant, he "humbled himself and became obedient unto death, even death on a cross."

In the service of anointing, representatives of Christ's body gather for the commissioning of one and the recommissioning of all to health.

We anoint and are anointed as an act of simple obedience, claiming the promise that wherever two or three gather in Christ's name, he is there in the midst with health-giving power.

We anoint and are anointed as an act of penitence, confessing that we all together need the forgiveness and the wholeness made possible by Christ's living spirit.

We anoint and are anointed as an act of petition, asking that we be renewed in the hope that holds firm even in those moments when we echo Christ's own lament, "My God, my God, why have you forsaken me?" the hope that permits us to know that even in the midst of suffering and pain we have been bound to God and each other by cords of compassion and ropes of love that nothing in all creation can ever tear apart.

We are cleansed by his obedience. We are commissioned and recommissioned by his cleansing, commissioned and recommissioned to extend his exchange in behalf of others and to receive the health intended by God's loving purpose.

Search Me, O God

O God, grant to each of us a larger measure of Christ's own obedience as those who receive and witness to your healing.

"O Lord, thou has searched me and known me! Thou knowest when I sit down and when I rise up; thou discernest my thoughts from afar. Thou searchest out my path and my lying down, and are acquainted with all my ways."

"Search me, O God, and know my heart! Try me and know my thoughts! And see if there be any wicked way in me, and lead me in the way everlasting!" (Psalm 139:1-3, 23-24). Amen.

25

BAPTISM

Baptized Into His Death

All of us who have been baptized into Christ Jesus were baptized into his death . . . so that as Christ was raised from the dead by the glory of the Father, we too might walk in newness of life" (Romans 6:3, 4).

"For our sake he made him to be sin who knew no sin, so that in him we might become the righteousness of God" (2 Corinthians 5:21).

These texts make it plain that Jesus' engagement with sin and death in our behalf was much more than mere play-acting, much more than make-believe suffering. The engagement was agonizingly real. Jesus fully shared our humanity with all its vulnerabilities, its struggles, even its most persistent temptations.

This is also what the Letter to the Hebrews says, and in a variety of ways. "For we have not a high priest who is unable to sympathize with our weakness, but one who in every respect has been tempted as we are, yet without sinning" (Hebrews 4:15).

"Sympathize with" is too weak a rendering of what this passage has in mind. Jesus faced temptations without sinning. This resulted not from the automatic consequences of his unique status as God's anointed or his divine nature, but from a real victory in the midst of an equally real struggle. Able to "sympathize with us in our weaknesses," yes! But not simply from a distance in merely attitudinal terms. Rather, he is a "high priest" who is able to stand with us in our present testings because he has been there ahead of us!

Jesus encountered sin and death in our behalf. He met a formidable enemy. "He himself partook of the same nature (the same humanity as our own), that through death he might destroy him who has the power of death, that is, the devil, and deliver all those who through fear of death were subject to lifelong bondage" (Hebrews 2:14).

His sufferings were intense. "In the days of his flesh Jesus offered up prayers and supplications, with loud cries and tears, to him who was able to save him from death, and he was heard for his godly fear. Although he was a Son, he learned obedience through what he suffered . . ."(Hebrews 5:7-8a).

At the beginning and throughout his ministry he was tested. He was tempted as one who experienced our humanity. He was tempted as the one who was uniquely God's anointed, as the one in whom God himself "became flesh and dwelt among us . . . and we have beheld his glory, glory as of the only Son from the Father"(John 1:14).

All this invites us to look quite closely at Jesus' temptations, which reached their sharpest points at the beginning of his ministry (in the wilderness) and also just prior to his crucifixion (Gethsemane).

Testing in the Wilderness: The Synoptic Gospels refer to Jesus' being led into the wilderness immediately following his baptism—Matthew and Luke giving the longer accounts with only a brief mention in Mark.

All agree that Jesus did not got into the wilderness to seek a place of retreat for prayer and contemplation. The wilderness was understood to be the very opposite of that place spoken of in our familiar hymn—"a place of quiet rest, near to the heart of God, a place where sin cannot molest." The wilderness is a setting of active conflict, where God seems distant, where sin can molest, where the devil, the ruler of the kingdom of darkness and death, holds sway.

Matthew 4:1ff. and Luke 4:1ff. speak of Jesus' being led into the wilderness by the Spirit. Mark 1:12f. puts it even stronger, saying that Jesus was driven by the Spirit into the wilderness to be tempted, actually put to the test. The reference to the Spirit leading, or driving, Jesus into the wilderness makes it clear that in the deepest sense his testing had something to do with God himself, although in a hidden way.

We encounter here an overlay of meanings. The Israelites wandered in the wilderness forty years, a place in which God's promise at best seemed insecure and at worst overwhelmed by other powers, a place in which the boundary lines blurred between the "truth" of God's steadfastness in covenant and the "lie" that we are better off when we take things into our own hands, a place of ambiguity close to the Promised Land yet still only on the edges, close to a gracious environment yet where the people of the promise were forced to wander as judgment upon their disobedience, a place that allows no escape from God and his purpose even when, through creaturely rebellion, sin and death seem more dominant than wholeness and life.

Into the wilderness Jesus went, led or driven there by the Spirit to be tested, a matter having to do not only with the devil but with God, though in a hidden way. At the end of the forty days, during which he ate nothing, Jesus was hungry. "The devil said to him, 'If you are the Son of God, command this stone to become bread.' And Jesus answered him, 'It is written, "We shall not live by bread alone"'" (Luke 4:3-4).

"And the devil took him up, and showed him all the kingdoms of the world in a moment of time, and said to him, 'To you I will give all this authority and their glory; for it has been delivered to me, and I give it to whom I will. If you, then, will worship me, it shall be yours.' And Jesus answered him, 'It is written, "You shall worship the Lord your God and him only shall you serve"'"(Luke 4:5-8).

Then the devil "took him to Jerusalem, and set him on the pinnacle of the temple, and said to him, 'If you are the Son of God, throw yourself down from there; for it is written, He will give his angels charge of you.' And Jesus answered him, 'It is said, "You shall not tempt the Lord your God"'" (Luke 4:9-12).

He was tempted as one who experienced our humanity to the fullest extent. He was tempted to exaggerate the importance of material things, forgetting that we need not be anxious, saying, "What shall we eat?" or "What shall we drink?" or "What shall we wear?" for the heavenly Father knows that we need them all! He was tempted to be preoccupied with worldly success and power, even if gained by compromise and misdirected worship, tempted to delight in sensationalism as an end in itself, forgetting that little is gained if we get the whole world and yet lose our lives.

He was tempted in every respect like us, and also as the One who was God's anointed, as the One in whom God himself became flesh and dwelt among us.

Aided by Karl Barth's interpretation of Jesus' temptations, we hear the Scriptures posing questions that now become ever more startling. Not merely will Jesus give in to the cunning of the devil by being preoccupied with material things, with worldly success and power, with sensationalism at whatever cost, but will Jesus be diverted from taking the offensive as only God's true anointed One can? Will he be diverted from his God-given mission to demonstrate what true creaturely dependence and penitence mean?

Yes, Jesus was tempted in all points as we are, only more so, for he was God's true anointed, for whom the testing went even beyond our own.

Jesus' Baptism by John. The wilderness temptations came immediately after Jesus' baptism by John—a baptism "with water for repentance."

By accepting baptism at the hands of this prophet, Jesus identified with John's call to repentance. He signaled acceptance of his unique mission to walk the way of the true penitent, the one who confesses what rebellious humankind from the fall of Adam and Eve onward has refused to confess, namely, that it is God, not man or woman, who judges between good and evil.

As God's anointed, Jesus is commissioned to take upon himself the role of the sinner repenting, yet without his sinning. In our place and in our behalf he is to confess that God alone has the right to rule. He is to counter the human delusion that we can be as God if we preserve the right to decide for ourselves, to take things into our own hands rather than obey God's command. He is to counter that sinful delusion by encountering it where it is strongest, in the wilderness where sin and death seem to have dominion. His temptation of temptations in the wilderness and later in Gethsemane is to shrink back from this calling with its struggles and anguish.

Testing in Gethsemane. Hebrews 5:7 says "In the days of his flesh, Jesus offered up prayers and supplications, with loud cries and tears . . . . " This text seems to have Jesus' conflict in Gethsemane in mind. In Gethsemane the cross looms before Jesus as an ominous threat. As God's anointed he would soon face the full consequences of his mission of penitence in our behalf, of his encounter with sin, death, law, and the devil.

Gethsemane brings Jesus to that ambiguous place in which the devil's power and God's power seem confused. He is to be handed over, required by his mission to give himself into the hands of sinners, of persons made violent by the delusion by which they and we live, the "lie" that things are better if we take control ourselves, if we (like Adam and Eve before us) set ourselves up as judges between good and evil rather than obey God as the true Judge.

Gethsemane for Jesus is the place in which the good intentions of God for his creation blur into the evil intentions of deluded persons and even of the devil himself. For here Jesus already anticipates the terror of the alienation from God that he is to bear on our behalf, "My God, my God, why have you forsaken me?"

Yet even in this place, the most hostile of environments, he confesses that God still has the right to rule.

In "agony he prayed more earnestly; and his sweat became like drops of blood falling down upon the ground" (Luke 22:44).

"Father, if you are willing, remove this cup from me; nevertheless, not my will, but yours, be done" (Luke 22:42).

Implications of Baptism for Daily Living. "He made him to be sin who knew no sin, so that in him we might become the righteousness of God." "Baptized into his death . . . so that as Christ was raised from the dead . . . we too might walk in newness of life." We are now in a better position to sense the utter realism of these strong affirmations of the Apostle Paul. Both texts have definite implications for daily living—so that we might become the righteousness of God and walk in newness of life.

Baptized into his death. That is what baptism is all about. It is a call to discipleship, a call based on an objective state of affairs that precedes our response. Jesus has encountered sin and death in our behalf. The enemy has been met precisely where he is the strongest. Jesus completed the mission of penitence and obedience begun in the wilderness.

Because this is so, being baptized into his death means bearing the mark of the cross, the mark of his grief and shame as the fitting expression of our discipleship. It means the enlargement of our sympathies and the freedom to extend Jesus' own penitence and obedience by taking our place amid human joy and sorrow, not forever doing battle with an already vanquished foe but being as those once dead but now raised to new life.

Hawthorne's well-known novel *The Scarlet Letter* is a parable of what it means to bear the mark of his death in our body. The tale is set in early New England with its Puritan standards and practices. It begins with Hester Prynne emerging from the town jail with a scarlet A sewn across her bosom. She committed an act of adultery while her husband was across the seas. The father of the child and her secret lover is Arthur Dimmesdale, the well-respected Puritan preacher in the village. Both Hester and Arthur wear a mark. Hester's is in the open for all to see, Arthur's a secret sign as part of his torturously kept secret.

Hester and Arthur seriously question whether to bear their "mark" in the midst of society or to find some avenue of flight. The forest on the edge of the settlement symbolizes the possibility of flight, of escape. But their momentary flight issues only in a return to the settlement. Arthur grows more and more tortured by his secret, and Hester becomes more and more an angel of mercy in the village.

In Hawthorne's novels one finds the view that apart from some "mark of grief" a person remains undeveloped, not fully a social being capable of sympathy and compassion. For example, he says of Pearl, the child born to Hester and Arthur as a living reminder of their forbidden moment of love in the forest, that she lacked "what some people want throughout life—a grief that should deeply touch her, and thus humanize and make her capable of sympathy."

As the story moves toward its end, Pearl receives this "mark of grief" through what amounts to the vicarious death of Arthur Dimmesdale after his tragic confession on the very scaffold that seven years before had witnessed the disgrace of Hester, his confession that he indeed is the child's father.

Arthur leaps to the scaffold and reveals his own concealed stigma, paralleling the scarlet A worn by Hester, a "mark" that over the years had come to stand less for adulteress and more for "able servant." In a similar way Arthur's stigma, even though a torturous secret, had seemingly developed in him an almost limitless capacity to identify with persons in their guilt and desperate need. At the time of Arthur's confession, Roger Chillingworth, Hester's husband, who has kept his identity secret in order to give himself over to a program of self-destroying vengeance, is greatly distressed.

In the closing dialog Roger addresses Arthur Dimmesdale on the scaffold:

"Thou hast escaped me," Roger Chillingworth repeated more than once. "Thou hast escaped me!"

"May God forgive thee!" said the minister. "Thou too hast deeply sinned!"

The minister withdrew his dying eyes from Chillingworth and fixed them on the woman and the child.

"My dear little Pearl," said he, feebly—and there was a sweet and gentle smile over his face, as of a spirit sinking into deep repose; nay, now that the burden was removed, it seemed almost as if he would be sportive with the child—"Dear little Pearl, wilt thou kiss me now? Thou wouldst not, yonder, in the forest! But now thou wilt!"

Pearl kissed his lips. A spell was broken. The great sense of grief, in which the wild infant bore a part, had developed all her sympathies; and as her tears fell upon her father's cheek, they were the pledge that she would grow up amid human joy and sorrow, nor forever do battle with the world, but be a woman in it.

Being baptized into Jesus' death evokes something no less dramatic and life changing than the "great scene of grief" that quickened Pearl's development. In fact, baptism as grounded in Jesus' actual victory in our behalf and as a call to active penitence and obedience means a great deal more. It means being called and set free to place ourselves at the disposal of God as those who were dead but raised to new life.

God in Jesus Christ has reached toward us and experienced life from our side as a means of restored communion with himself and the world that he loves. In Jesus' penitence and obedience in our behalf, in his death on the cross and his victorious resurrection, we have God's own "living word" made flesh penetrating our blindness and deafness, giving us light, hope, joy, setting us free, free to walk the way of penitence and obedience, free since "all who have been baptized into Christ Jesus were baptized into his death . . . so that as Christ was raised from the dead by the glory of the Father, we too might walk in newness of life."

On Walking With Head Held High and a Quickened Step

O God, you know that the cares and distractions of life are always with us, so grant us the gift of attentiveness in these moments of prayer.

We voice the needs and concerns of the heart, not because they are not already known to you but because we have been taught by Christ to pray even for our daily bread and because even now Christ is seated at your right hand interceding for us.

We confess that we do not heed Jesus' admonition to "watch and pray with him." Like the eyes of the disciples in the Garden of Gethsemane, our eyes grow heavy; we sleep; we let Jesus pray alone.

But we praise you that Jesus prays in our place and in our behalf, and so we continue in our daily walk, renewed in the desire to follow after Jesus, who has shown us what it means to say "thank you, God," and then to live out that thankfulness in pursuit of your kingdom and the neighbor's good. Amen.

26
BIRTHDAYS

Remembering Who We Are!

Birthdays are very special times. As individuals, though, we may feel ambivalent about them. We like the gatherings of family and friends with the many expressions of love and good wishes. But as one year follows another, each seeming to go faster than the one before, we are tempted to join Jack Benny in fantasizing that we are 39-and-holding. Some of us, like myself, may even be traumatized the first time we are offered a senior citizen's discount for a restaurant meal.

As institutions, as denominations, we are less uncertain about advancing age. The Church of the Brethren, this year, is 275 years old. We state that boldly. We celebrate it.

In any case, whether of individuals or of a denomination, birthdays are opportunities for renewed commitment to one another and to the things that matter most.

Therefore, may this 275th anniversary year that is closing be a time of recommitment to our founding vision and guiding purpose; may it be a time when Brethren heed the admonition of Paul Hoffman, which he made during his annual conference moderator's address: "Not to stew about our past, but to move within the New Testament in whatever way God leads!" Or, to be guided—in fitting ways—by our heritage and by God's promise!

Growing up as I did in Harleysville, Pennsylvania, a son of parents with deep roots in both Mennonite and Brethren communities, centered in the Pennsylvania Dutch culture, I was occasionally given specific instruction about fitting behavior: Don't dawdle after school! When you do a thing, do it right! Don't waste food; clean your plate! Wipe your shoes before coming into the house! Walk, don't run! Don't be so *Rutschlich*! so *Doppich*! so *Wunnerfitslich*!

More often, instruction came by a simple admonition. The occassions evoking this admonition were varied: returning to school after receiving a chipped front tooth during a playground scuffle, taking out the family car for a Saturday evening with other teen-age friends, boarding the train to go to New York City to attend evening high school and a Bible institute, later marrying and enrolling at Juniata, Bethany, and Yale. The simple admonition came repeatedly on such occasions: "Remember who you are!"

Somehow for my parents that said it all. And in a very real way it did. "Remembering who I was"—a member of a particular household, the son of particular parents, belonging to a particular neighborhood and to particular church communities—had a great deal to do with my sense of fitting actions, with my vision of future possibilities and life directions.

This applies equally to the Church of the Brethren during this 275th anniversary year. "Mission" receives its charter and its goal from "identity." We fittingly respond to the challenge of the next quarter century and beyond, with its threats and its promises, by gratefully and obediently "remembering who we are."

We respond not merely as individual moral agents who act in

terms of duties and principles, means and ends, and perceptions of the right and the good. We are such agents and do determine our actions on such terms, but not merely so!

We respond not merely as members of American society with its self-understandings, its fears and certainties, its dominant behavior patterns and cultural tendencies. We are members of American society and are shaped by it, but not merely so!

Nor do we respond merely as members of the Church of the Brethren with the distinctive memories and aspirations of this one faith community among the many others that make up the church universal. We are Brethren and do so respond, but not merely so!

We are heirs of the promise God first made to Abraham and Sarah: through them "were born descendants as many as the stars of heaven and as the innumerable grains of sand by the seashore" (Hebrews 11:12). Like Abraham and Sarah and all their heirs we are called to respond to God's promise and God's command, to be on a journey of faith and obedience, to acknowledge that our very life as persons and as a people is a gift gratefully to be received, and with humility to confess our need of empowerment, of penitence, and of renewal every step along the way.

We gain inspiration and guidance from that "great cloud of witnesses" who in every age make up this pilgrim people. These witnesses include the many participants in the unfolding histories of Israel and the church.

While commending many of these faithful witnesses, the writer of Hebrews blurts out that time would fail him to tell of all those "who through faith conquered kingdoms, enforced justice, received promises, stopped the mouths of lions, quenched raging fires, escaped the edge of the sword, won strength out of weakness" (Hebrews 11:33-34a). So time would fail me to tell of all those who through the centuries have obeyed when Christ Jesus said, "Count well the cost."

Our recital of those who have "counted well the cost" would have to include: the "eight brothers and sisters who made that bold move 275 years ago, separating themselves from the established church in Germany, risking persecution, loss of home and property, even loss of life itself;" the "Solingen Six," early Brethren who were imprisoned for their faith from 1717 to 1720, all the while writing hymns and singing when they could get together, and saying of this time of testing, "We did not fear any man, because Jesus, his truth and teaching, were our protection and solace;" Sarah Major who kept preaching even when the annual meeting of 1834 said, "To allow a woman to preach is 'not approved of;'" Nettie Senger, the twentieth-century missionary who in spite of hardships and frustrations "loved all her work in China, because 'God works for good.'"

Surrounded by many who are indeed "well attested in their faith," "let us also lay aside every weight, and sin which clings so closely, and let us run with perseverance the race that is set before us, looking to Jesus the pioneer and perfecter of our faith" (Hebrews 12:1b-2).

We center our confidence not in ourselves, but in the One who endured the shame of a criminal's death on the cross, and, even more, the unthinkable threat and agony of bearing humanity's alienation from God: "My God, my God, why have you forsaken me?"

In running "with perseverance the race that is set before us," we receive our endurance and our direction from Jesus Christ. He is, and he represents to us, the simple reality of God, whose power is at the same time grace, whose love is also justice, whose justice is a plumbline that unerringly marks the path of truth, whose gift of new life requires dying to old patterns. "For as grains of wheat before they grow are buried in the earth below, so too must we from sin and self be free."

In Christ we receive that gift of new life, of freedom from sin and self, freedom from expecting too little or too much from ourselves, too little or the wrong things from God, freedom to face even life's deepest threats and contradictions strengthened by the confidence that "in Christ all things are held together."

If we are to "move within the New Testament in whatever way God leads," where else can we turn than to Jesus Christ, in whom all things hold together? He is God's no when we are too despairing and too optimistic; he is God's no when we expect too little or too much of ourselves, and when we expect too little or the wrong things of God. He is God's no to continuing human rebellion and disorder, whose boundary limits are now clearly marked by the cross and the empty tomb. He is God's no because he is God's yes pronounced on all God's promises, every one of them!

In this 275th anniversary year let us "remember who we are!" We are those who "follow after Jesus." "For to this you have been called, because Christ suffered for you, leaving you an example, that you should follow in his steps" (1 Peter 2:21). This text still speaks plainly to us. *Nachfolge!* Following after Jesus! Radical discipleship! That is our identity that "stirs us to build new worlds in Christ's name," that charts the direction of our continuing pilgrimage!

Not only called but also empowered! Not merely for outward imitation, for external copying, but for a life of grateful obedience based on Christ's prior initiative. "We are not asked to seek the way. The way has come to us. We have but to rise and walk!"

Called and empowered! We need not climb the heavenly steeps

to bring the Lord Christ down. Because the "Word became flesh and walked among us," we may live by simple trust like those who heard beside the Syrian Sea; we may take the next step without knowing all that remains ahead except God's promise, "I shall be your God; you shall be my people."

Called and empowered! "In the fight against sin we have not yet had to keep fighting to the point of death, and if we think of the way Jesus stood such opposition from sinners, then we shall not give up for want of courage."

Called and empowered! To witness by deed and not only by words to "having died with Christ so that we might also be raised with him." That witness may be faithful stewardship of gifts and resources in building up the worshiping-serving church of Jesus Christ. It may be finding compelling ways to express the heartfelt conviction that "we've a story to tell to the nations, that shall turn our hearts to the right."

It may be support of a Catholic Bishop's "Pastoral Letter" urging active peacemaking in response to the nuclear threat. It may be conscientious objection to or noncooperation with the draft, war tax resistance, or some form of alternative service.

All such actions are signs that we are continuing with boldness on our journey of faith and obedience. And so let us lean toward the "moving years and marching days" still ahead, knowing that even when the path is dark and threatening, we can take refuge in God's steadfast promise.

That promise is "to us better than a light or any known way." We need not settle for illusory rest stops that offer only false security. We may be strong in Christ's prior obedience and in the manifold gifts of Christ's Spirit. Looking ahead by looking back, let us seek by God's grace to live the life of the One we nailed upon the tree. For then all creation is filled with promise, its claim to confidence as certain as the truth that sets us free! Amen.

—Reprinted from *Messenger*, December 1983, Vol. 132, Number 12.

The Grace of Remembering Who We Are

O God, we confess our need for the grace of remembering who we are, for truly we need daily strengthening and direction in our calling.

Help us go forward even when the tasks seem overwhelming, when the path before us is dark and ominous.

Spur us onward in the race when we are tempted to give up for want of courage.

Empower us to answer the call of Jesus, who leads us in our faith and brings it to perfection, so that we too shall arrive, as strangers and sojourners, in the Promised Land and have the forward-leaning patience to live there as in a strange country, still looking toward "that city which has a foundation, whose builder and maker is God." Amen.

27

CHURCH RENEWAL

Heirs According to Promise

Throughout the church I sense a very earnest yearning, an often unspoken but heartfelt prayer, not for lifeless uniformity, but for life-giving unity in the "one body and the one Spirit," for focus and renewal in the midst of divergent expressions of faith and life as a people. Our unspoken prayer is that we will be grasped compellingly with power for new faithfulness by the God who is the very source of life itself.

Galatians speaks directly to this corporate yearning for focus and renewal. "For as many of you as were baptized into Christ have put on Christ. There is neither Jew nor Greek, there is neither slave nor free, there is neither male nor female; for you are all one in Christ Jesus. And if you are Christ's, then you are Abraham's offspring, heirs according to promise" (Galatians 3:27-29).

The "heirs" mentioned here are the Gentiles: those who were "separated from Christ, alienated from the commonwealth of Israel, and strangers to the covenants of promise, having no hope and without God in the world" (Ephesians 2:12); those who are "no longer strangers and sojourners but [cocitizens] with the saints and members of the household of God . . . members of the same body, and partakers of the promise in Christ Jesus through the gospel" (Ephesians 2:19; 3:6).

The question being addressed in Galatians is whether Gentiles may join the church without first being circumcised. The answer is clear and straight-forward. You do not have to become a Jew first to become a Christian. There is direct access to Christ for Gentiles apart from the law. For the relationship is centered in God's promise to Abraham and Sarah, through whom all the nations would be blessed and who themselves were counted as righteous not in terms of "works of law" but of "faith."

The law was a "custodian." The Greek word is *paidagogos*. The reference is not to a superior teacher such as we imply when speaking of a "pedagogue." A *paidagogos* is often described in Greek comedies and on Roman reliefs as a "harsh, uneducated slave who, for example holds a little school boy a couple of inches above the ground by his ear." With that in mind Krister Stendahl suggests that the law served "as a harsh babysitter to see to it that the children of Israel did not raid the refrigerator before the great party at which the Gentiles should also be present." In this way, "what was promised to faith in Jesus Christ might be given to those who believe" (Galatians 3:22).

The "custodian's" service lasted only "until Christ came." That temporal limit is joyful news. "For all who rely on works of the law are under a curse; for it is written, 'Cursed be every one who does not abide by all things written in the book of the law, and do them'" (Galatians 3:10). But "Christ redeemed us from the curse of the law, having become a curse for us—for it is written, 'Cursed be every one who hangs on a tree'—that in Christ Jesus the blessing of Abraham [and Sarah] might come upon the Gentiles, that we might receive the promise of the Spirit through faith" (Galatians 3:13-14).

"Life in the promise" is superior to "life under the law," for the heir as long as he or she is legally bound is no better than a slave. Such an heir is still under guardians or trustees until a date set by the parent. "Children under the law" have precisely that subordinate status, but "children of the promise" do not. "When the time had fully come, God sent forth his Son, born of a woman, born under the law, to redeem those who were under the law, so that we might receive adoption as sons [and daughters] . . . God has sent the Spirit of his Son into our hearts, crying, 'Abba! Father!' So through God you are no longer a slave but a son [or a daughter], and . . . then an heir" (Galatians 4:4-7).

No theme is more dominant throughout the Scriptures than that of "promise." Think of the qualities of a promise: invisible, with no obvious force at its disposal, seemingly quite fragile in face of obstacles, yet potentially very powerful. A promise may deeply motivate and direct activities. As a boy, I washed dishes without complaint for a whole month before Christmas because of a promise about receiving a favorite toy as long as Santa received a good report. I stop whatever I am doing, however interesting, to meet my wife, Ruth, at the shopping center because I promised to be there, and she stops her search for a new dress because she promised to meet me at a certain time.

There is a promise at the center of the Scriptures—God's promise made to Abraham and Sarah, a promise to create a people out of wayfarers and outcastes, those who in themselves were "no people." Yet, how difficult it is to live obediently, joyously, adventurously in the strength of that promise.

When ninety-nine-year-old Abraham heard God say that he was

to be the "father of a multitude of nations" and that Sarah was to bear a son and become a "mother of nations," he could only fall on his face and laugh (Genesis 17:17).

When Sarah overheard what was said, she also laughed, saying in great disbelief, "Shall I indeed bear a child now that I am old?" (Genesis 18:13b).

When the Israelites were camped in the wilderness on the very edge of the Promised Land, ten of the leaders sent to spy out the land could not serve as true witnesses to the reliability of God's promise. Instead of God's power they saw only the might of their enemies. The Canaanites with their armor and strongholds and their advanced methods of warfare seemed to the desert nomads truly giants before whom they were mere grasshoppers.

God's promise is an active, creative power that persists even in the face of foolish, fear-ridden, prideful, unbelieving, disobedient actions. God wills life, yes, "new life." Jeremiah understood that: "Behold, the days are coming, says the Lord, when I will make a new covenant [reestablish the original promise]. . . . I will put my law within them, and I will write it upon their hearts, and I will be their God, and they shall be my people . . . . They shall all know me, from the least of them to the greatest" (Jeremiah 31:31-34).

The Apostle Paul also understood that God wills "new life." No longer under the harsh tutelage of the "law written on tablets of stone," we are freed for "life in the promise," which inwardly constrains us "to be servants of one another" (Galatians 5:13) and issues in the "fruit of the Spirit"—"love, joy, peace, patience, kindness, goodness, faithfulness, gentleness, self-control" (Galatians 5:22-23).

Paul's writings constantly presuppose Israel's prior responses to God's promise. But the accent shifts: less upon the Promised Land with its shadow side of conquest by military powers, and more upon the Promised Person, Jesus Christ, God's own anointed. In Christ's obedience we look for strength not in marching armies, but in the servant's role so powerfully enacted when Jesus "poured water into a basin, and began to wash the disciples' feet, and to wipe them with the towel with which he was girded" (John 13:5). In Christ's obedience "all the promises of God find their yes," their personal validation, for through Christ "he has put his seal upon us and has given us his Spirit in our hearts as a guarantee" (2 Corinthians 1:20-22). In Christ's obedience faith is quickened, for God's promise has not been overcome by darkness, by principalities and powers, not even by death itself—that most formidable enemy, that "giant of giants" before whom the "children of the promise" need no longer flee like timid, skittish grasshoppers.

In the strength of that victorous promise we are assured of belonging in God's household. That belonging centers not in our own righteousness but in Christ, who "redeemed us from the curse of the law, having become a curse for us. . . . " Therefore we have the full status of sons and daughters and may address God as "Abba! Father!" He is the one who loves with the full devotion of a heavenly parent, who understands the frustrations and temptations, the scrapes and scars of his children as though his very own.

Some years ago an event occurred on the sidewalk just outside the former Bethany Theological Seminary campus on Van Buren Street in Chicago. Our son David, then about two years old, was walking beside me when he stumbled and fell. He picked himself up with indignation on his face and proceeded to vent his feelings of outrage by kicking me in the shins.

The God we address as "Abba!" is identified with our frailties in a direct and personal way. God knows our tendency to stumble and fall and is on the receiving end of our kicks of frustration as only God can be!

That same gracious God also "sent forth his Son, born of woman, . . . to redeem those who were under the law . . . ," even though a rebellious people was sure to misinterpret the Son's mission and put him to death. With this central gospel affirmation, what a "strange new world" we enter. For could any earthly parent even consider such an action? Who else but God could love like that?

God's "immortal love, forever full, forever flowing free," is the foundation of the household in which we belong—an inclusive household. In that household "there is neither Jew nor Greek, there is neither slave nor free, there is neither male nor female;" for all are "one in Christ Jesus" (Galatians 3:28).

There membership is gained not in the strength of our good works but solely by God's invitation and actions in our behalf.

There the well-being of the whole body, of the whole household, remains the uppermost concern of all members. For membership in the household brings with it rights, privileges, and duties.

Steve Douglas, you will recall, is the ideal "father" in "My Three Sons" who never seems to be flustered by any family crisis. The three sons are Robbie, the eldest, Chip, the middle one, and Ernie, the youngest—actually just recently "adopted" into the household.

In one episode Steve was getting ready for his annual first-day trout-fishing trip with Robbie. This was time not only for matching wits with native rainbows, but also for "father" and "eldest son" conversation. Steve was eager for the day. Robbie was less enthusiastic because of a prospective date with a new girlfriend.

The family tradition was clear: father fishing on the day with eldest son; eventually it would be Chip's turn; then Ernie's. But Ernie didn't want to wait. He tried everything to be included in the fishing venture, even to taking Robbie's place.

Robbie tried to persuade his father to take Ernie instead of him. But Steve persisted. When pressed, Steve explained that Ernie's time would come. A family has its privileges but also its orderly rhythms, and if they were to make an exception for Ernie, they would really be treating him as a "guest," not as a full, contributing "member" of the household.

In a follow-up breakfast conversation Ernie confides, "I guess I do belong to this family, because they treat me like all the rest!"

We are adopted sons and daughters in God's household. We do not establish our own belonging. It is a free gift. Nor do we determine who else belongs. God's household includes all partners in creation, the distant neighbor as well as the neighbor close at hand, those already richly blessed and those yet excluded from the full rights and privileges of the one family.

Christ has freed us from the harsh custodianship of the law. But don't be deceived. God will not listen to our childish clamorings for special exceptions. God "treats us like all the rest." We are not "guests" but "responsible members" of the household. Therefore "do not use your freedom as an opportunity for the flesh, but through love be servants of one another. For the whole law is fulfilled in one word, 'You shall love your neighbor as yourself'" (Galatians 5:13-14). Obedience to that law of the new covenant is not a way of earning our place in the family, but a fitting response of mature sons and daughters.

As "heirs according to promise" we "live in the Spirit," and so "let us walk in the Spirit." Then we shall know the joy of our belonging. Amen.

—Adapted from "Heirs According to Promise," *Brethren Life and Thought*, Winter, 1980.

28

ECUMENICAL WORSHIP AND SERVICE

A Vision of Unity

Unity is central, not peripheral, to the church's life and mission, to its faith development and sharing. It is an essential part of what God intends for creation as this intention is revealed in Jesus

Christ and is being undergirded by Christ's living Spirit.

We have been paying insufficient attention to this mark of faithfulness. "Unity concerns" have often become associated with "ecumenical structures and programs," which have recently come under constant criticism. In a recent list of possible goals and priority objectives for the church, members of one denomination placed very near the bottom an objective to clarify its ecumenical posture for this decade. Other features of its heritage received more attention: peace, simple life, discipleship, family stability, personal and community integrity, servanthood, and a view of Scripture as the "infallible rule of faith and practice." It remembered its origins in terms of "breaking away" from the established churches in search of a more radical return to New Testament and early church patterns. It overlooked the extent to which it separated from mainline groups because of its strong emphasis upon "unity in the body" as a primary value, not to the neglect of, but also not set aside by, concern for right doctrines and properly administered sacraments.

What we urgently need is a vision of unity. It is part of a continuing ecumenical quest, a quest that is an original and fitting expression of our call to discipleship. It is a witness to the faith and hope we have been given through our specific history. It is also a heartfelt desire to be newly responsive to the Spirit's leading by being attentive to the Scriptures and to the ways scriptural teaching and promptings have shaped our corporate life.

Some foundational convictions about the nature of the church and the life of believers can help us listen afresh to the Scriptures and our Christian heritage as we reflect on church unity as a life to be lived.

Church Membership Means Being Grafted into Christ's Resurrection Body

Membership in the church means more than joining one voluntary agency among others in our society. It is like the relationship between a branch and the life-giving vine, or between an arm and the total organism through which the arm lives and acts.

Christians traditionally have understood the Scriptures to be speaking quite realistically in such ways of describing membership.

Believer's baptism has been so important for some groups because it is a "sign" of being incorporated into Christ's death and resurrection, of receiving the gift of a new identity, and of mature commitment to act in ways befitting one's new existence and allegiance to Christ as Lord.

This new identity is radical and transforming. It transcends all other identities: of natural and extended families, of colleague relations, of neighborhood, of country, even of a particular denominational grouping.

This new identity in simple and direct terms is becoming followers after Jesus, his disciples, who receive life in the midst of thankful obedience. Our new identity is to belong to those who follow Christ's example.

Early leaders in the Church of the Brethren stressed this new identity. Alexander Mack, Sr., wrote, "The baptism of Jesus by John is a great miracle and a great self-humiliation of the Son of God. He has left this to us and all his followers as a mighty example in which we should follow him."

Peter Nead likewise wrote, "Jesus Christ is our great example, and it becometh us to pattern after him—to walk in his footsteps. . . . If we have the spirit of Christ, we shall be meek and lowly of heart; and then it is that our walk and conduct will testify that we are children of God."

Cautions have appropriately been raised about the constant accent upon "doing as Jesus did," upon "following in his steps," and upon "seeking the mind of Christ in all things."

What must be remembered is that "Christ calls us to obedience, not merely to outward imitation." And this obedience, which is the arm of Christ's saving work, involves more than external copying. It is based on Christ's prior initiatives.

Peter Miller added some comments to the writing *Scriptural Vindication* by Alexander Mack, Jr. He stated, "Our obedience has its possibility in the household of the New Covenant . . . in which obedience is rendered not by the lesser to the greater (as in the household of Moses) but by the greater to the lesser. The foundation of this household was laid by Christ when he was baptized in the Jordan by John, who was lesser than he."

Miller continues, "Just as the chief high priest pledged himself to the Father through his baptism to make the entire rebelling creation subject to him, so all of his followers with their baptism have pledged themselves by oath to him to assist him in this important task. That is why Peter calls them a royal priesthood" (1 Peter 2:9).

The innocent suffering and good deeds of believers serve as visible signs of their promise to share Christ's mission (1 Peter 2:20-21). Through active discipleship, through obedience that corresponds to and is empowered by Jesus' prior obedience, the rebellious creation is gaining release from its "futile ways" (1 Peter 1:18).

Through the active discipleship of Jesus' followers the world is being delivered from its hostility to the way of Christ. Paul S. Minear has commented helpfully on John 17. This passage contains Jesus' prayer "that they may all be one . . . so that the world may know that thou hast sent me and hast loved them even as thou hast loved me" (John 17:21a and 23b). The "world," here and elsewhere in John, Minear notes, is not to be identified with others than ourselves, or we become hypocritical and blind like the Pharisees and priests. The "world" is not merely our customary notions of the physical universe, the human race, cultures, or unbelieving outsiders. It refers to a "massive, cohesive reality that becomes manifest in hostility to Christ and his disciples." The "world" is under the rulership of the "Father of Lies" not the Father of the Lord Jesus Christ. It lacks the peace, joy, hope, and victory that Christ offers. It is unable to see or know the truth or to receive the Spirit that sets us free.

"That they may all be one" is a call for newness of life, not just for changing organizational patterns. It is a call for oneness in the love of Jesus for the world—in us and around us—that still reflects hostility to the way of Christ. It is a call to unity, to mission, to evangelistic witness, to faith sharing. As followers after Jesus, in our unity and our obedience we are to give visible form to the world being delivered from its hostility to Christ. That is the belief and knowledge for which Jesus prays—"so that the world may believe that thou hast sent me . . . so that the world may know that thou hast sent me and hast loved them even as thou hast loved me" (John 17:21b, 23b).

The Church is a Fellowship of Discipline and Authority

The denominational polity of the Church of the Brethren has consistently included interconnectional patterns. From its earliest beginnings congregations were linked for edification, discipline, ordinances, and counsel. In 1723 the Germantown Brethren consulted European Brethren before baptizing members. By 1742 the practice began of holding Big Meetings to deal with matters of procedure, polity, program, and guidance. In 1856 district organizational structures evolved.

Implicit in these polity provisions is the view that the vigor and faithfulness of the church requires open interchange between accountable groupings, for wherever "two or three gather in Christ's name" they fittingly "search the Scriptures together; they seek the mind of Christ for corporate and individual guidance."

Implicit also is a strong ecumenical challenge, a forceful reminder that there indeed is "one body and one Spirit, one hope that belongs to our call, one Lord, one faith, one baptism, one God who is above all and in all" (Ephesians 4:4ff.). For these polity structures point beyond the boundaries of any single denominational body.

The scripturally based urgings that led to these polity directions have also propelled Brethren toward active conciliar involvements. And Brethren quickly sense that such cooperative relationships and undertakings are important not merely for efficiency in accomplishing tasks but for the sake of mutual edification and challenge so the church experiences "bodily growth and upbuilds itself in love" (Ephesians 4:16b).

Cooperation among church families is for communion, not a means of escape from deepened covenants and mutual commitments. Otherwise, cooperation becomes a stage in which churches are "not quite divided while remaining far from united," to quote a 1978 statement of the World Council of Churches.

Even in their brokenness and partiality ecumenical gatherings and shared ventures are "signs" of the church's true nature as a fellowship of discipline and authority. As such, the church is something like a strong family assembled in council for mutual challenge, discernment, and decisions whose claims on the members are stronger than those arrived at by conferral in nonauthoritative settings.

The Annual Conference of the Church of the Brethren foreshadows the church as such an authoritative fellowship. At times, Annual Conference is that—a conference and no more. We confer, consult and receive such advice as may commend itself to us and the congregations we represent. We write and discuss papers on a variety of topics and in the process separate those who believe this from those who believe that. All too often we also seem merely "not quite divided while remaining far from united."

Occasionally, however, perhaps even in the midst of our deepest disagreements, we catch fleeting glimpses of what it is like to be a family in council. We work to resolve problems, disagreements, and conflicts in the spirit of solidarity and acceptance of genuine differences that are not glossed over. We sense that we participate in an authoritative fellowship of shared life and decision making. We discuss and act in terms of covenants and commitments that bind us. We "speak the truth in love" to one another, and we strive to "maintain the unity of the Spirit in the bond of peace."

Then Annual Conference, by a grace and wisdom beyond our own, becomes a "sign" of the larger church as a fellowship of discipline and authority, a provisional realization of that day when the separated church families can gather in true council. Then we begin to understand ourselves as a family of families, a communion of communions in that new community of Christ's Spirit. Then we confess that our divided church families serve only as temporary way stations.

Without compromising our truest beliefs we look toward and work for that day when the distinctive gifts of each church family shall be trully named and fulfilled in Christ's new corporate existence.

We Belong at the Lord's Table in the Strength of God's Invitation and on God's Terms, Not Our Own

For Brethren the Love Feast and Communion service is lodged in the midst of congregational life and worship. Around this important ordinance cluster our firmest liturgical understandings and beliefs about the nature of the church and the life of the believer.

This lively symbol reminds us that God does indeed walk among us, that God's abode is a manger, a basin and a towel, a cross, an empty tomb.

When we wash the feet of our neighbor and allow our own feet to be washed, we are renewed in evangelism and mission, and we are urged onward in the ecumenical quest. We both give and receive. We are told again what we are so prone to forget—that life is to be gained not by lording it over others but by serving and being served.

When we share in the fellowship meal, we proclaim by that very act that the church is a fellowship of authority and discipline whose source is God's own love and mercy. In such an authoritative fellowship we are bound to one another in covenants and commitments that point beyond our immediate circle, that prefigure an ever-widening circle of care, insight, and mutual accountability.

When we partake of the bread and cup, we are admonished to stir up the gift of God that is in us because we have been baptized and incorporated into Christ's death and resurrection, and because we participate in the new community of Christ's Spirit.

We gather at the table of the Lord not in the strength of our merit but of God's grace. There all are seated not by special human invitation, as though we did not belong, but by virtue of being God's people, God's family.

Brethren lean heavily on the family analogy for understanding the nature of the church. We cherish the denominational image and experience of being like an "extended family." We take great delight in the familiar ritual of greeting each other with eager inquiries about possible family connections. The Lord's table is a plumbline in our midst, judging our perpetual drift toward clannishness, toward anxious preoccupation with "our own kind," toward subtle forms of exclusiveness.

Without exception all who gather at the Lord's table do so by virtue of membership in God's family. Here persons belong like children at a family meal. They belong and are expected to express that belonging in fitting ways.

But we confess and are humbled by the realization that not all Christians can share this common meal. This indicates the ecumenical pathos that touches us all.

Even the church's strongest symbols of unity have become divisive. The church thereby also reflects the brokenness of the larger human community. Persons outside the church do not feel welcome at the Lord's table. And yet the symbol remains, and every time we share in the Love Feast and Communion, we do so in anticipation of the messianic banquet. For then indeed the "Lord will be King on all the earth; on that day the Lord will be one and the Lord's name one" (Zechariah 14:9). Then our beginnings in God's ultimate purpose will be fully united with our new beginnings in Christ, whose "name is above every name, that at the name of Jesus every knee should bow, in heaven and on earth, and under the earth, and every tongue confess that Jesus Christ is Lord" (Philippians 2:9b-11a).

That the Church May Be One

O God, by your great mercy and wisdom give us the breadth of vision and the depth of compassion and penitence that will enable us to "speak the truth in love," in keeping with the faith and hope that is within us, so that we will be your obedient servants in "maintaining the unity of the Spirit in the bond of peace." *Ecumene!* The church is one. So let it be! Amen.

("The Vision of Unity for the Church of the Brethren in the 1980s" that was adopted by the Wichita Annual Conference as recorded in the *196th Church of the Brethren Annual Conference Minutes—1982* drew upon the directions and some specific phrases that were part of this address, first given at the Annual Conference Ecumenical Luncheon, June 24, 1981.)

29

FACING AN UNCERTAIN FUTURE

Take No Thought for the Morrow

When I was about a fourth and fifth grader attending Sunday school, I was given Scripture memory verses on little blue cards. After I could recite a sufficient number of them, I earned red cards, and enough red cards secured for me a brand new Bible.

Two of these childhood memory verses were Matthew 6:33 and 34:

> But seek ye first the kingdom of God, and his righteousness; and all these things shall be added unto you.
>
> Take therefore no thought for the morrow, for the morrow shall take thought for the things of itself. Sufficient unto the day is the evil thereof.

"Take no thought for the morrow!" Not for your life. Not for what you eat or drink or wear. Consider the fowls of the air and the lilies of the field. God cares for them. How much more will you be cared for? God knows your every need even before you do. So why take thought for the morrow, for the morrow will take thought for the things of itself!

I memorized the verses on my blue cards before I felt the startling impact of what they were saying to me. But from very early on, and ever since, I have been puzzled by the instruction that we are to "take no thought for the morrow."

Those who know me best will testify that this admonition calls for a response almost totally alien to my strongest dispositions. I like to plan and prepare well in advance. I give a great deal of forethought to many things relating to my work at Bethany Seminary and in the church—a new academic year, syllabi and other matters relating to courses I am scheduled to teach, institutional budgeting and overall development, continuing and newly emerging seminary programs, agenda for the board of directors, leadership needs of the denomination, writing projects, meditations, and sermons.

Nearly a month before it was scheduled, I shared with a colleague a preliminary sketch of a sermon I was preparing. She listened politely, and then with characteristic discernment asked, "Warren, why are you preparing so far ahead?"

Every time I am confronted by today's Scripture passage, my puzzlement returns. Something wells up from deep within me insisting that to take no thought for the morrow is most impractical

—highly imprudent!

Yet an event occurred recently to make me ponder whether the Scriptures on this point might actually reflect more prudential wisdom than I have typically assumed. We were on the Pennsylvania turnpike near Carlisle, returning from the Annual Conference of the Church of the Brethren, driving in the left lane at the speed limit when without any warning the right rear tire blew out. The noise was such that we thought a highway patrol helicopter was monitoring our speed by flying close enough to record our speedometer. The problem soon became apparent. But by the time the car could be slowed down and wended safely across traffic to stop on the right side of the road, the tire was shredded.

What you also need to know is that this tire was nearly brand new. On the very day we left for Annual Conference in Baltimore I had four new Goodyear steel belted radial tires put on our 1975 Le Sabre. This was part of my overall pretrip preparation and my attempt to avoid precisely what occurred—a blowout en route. The replaced tires were starting to show wear, although they were not yet so worn as to be unusable.

Amidst repeated expressions of disbelief that this could happen to a new tire, on the rest of the trip home I began asking myself, "Could taking thought about the morrow be carried too far? In taking extra precautions might we sometimes bring on the very adverse situations we are trying to avoid?"

Other memories have since fanned the flames of my questioning. Each year I work to get Annual Conference housing information as early as possible. I promptly send our particular housing request to the housing bureau and also immediately share the information with faculty and staff colleagues. But now that I think about it, in four or so out of the last six years my forethought has not produced the desired results. Other colleagues who seem much more nonchalant about getting in their request and advance deposit hear from the housing bureau earlier than we do—and get their first choices. We receive our confirmation late and often find that final arrangements do not quite match what we requested.

Then there was the time in the early 1960s when in the month of January I needed to travel to New York City to attend the meeting of a church-sponsored study committee. It being January and quite wintry, my thoughts about the morrow led me to travel by train rather than by plane, deeming that to be safer. But you guessed it. That New York Central was derailed that very day. While there were no serious injuries, it was one of the most uncomfortable, even most dangerous, of the trips I had ever taken by commercial means.

In the light of these remembered incidents I am now faced with the temptation to replace long-standing puzzlement with this principle based on prudential considerations: Better to think too little rather than too much about the morrow lest you make things worse!

But would such a principle really be serviceable? Would I be less likely to get another blowout on the Pennsylvania turnpike if I became less observant about the amount of tread remaining on our tires? Would the Groffs be more sure to get their desired Annual Conference housing accommodations if I waited longer to send in our request? Would I be safer if I gave less forethought to the better way to travel commercially when weather conditions are especially hazardous?

By simply posing such questions we all quickly sense that a calculated lack of planning, of preparedness, of forethought is too simple a reaction. A nervous manipulation of the future has its problems. But so does a casual abnegation of responsibility.

So any principle based on prudential wisdom would need to go something like this: Better to think neither too much nor too little about the morrow lest you make things worse!

But does that adequately hear what the Scriptures would have us hear? No, it does not! "Take therefore no thought about the morrow" shifts the very ground on which we stand. It requires that we see with new eyes, that we be converted, that we reason from the transforming perspective of Kingdom wisdom. "Seek ye first the kingdom of God and his righteousness; and all these things shall be added unto you."

From this transforming perspective I am constrained, and so are we all, to replace puzzlement not with a prudentially derived principle but with a person, the person of Jesus Christ, the very embodiment of this Sermon on the Mount teaching, the powerful, personal presence of the "kingdom of God and his righteousness," the very kingdom we are admonished to seek.

Because Jesus Christ, the crucified-risen Lord, has become the "way, the truth, and the life," we are called to and empowered for a freedom the world neither knows nor imagines,

> —freedom from all manner of worldly preoccupations: possessions, fame, in-group protectiveness, daily sustenance, personal and national security, even academic and professional attainments;
> —freedom from idolatrous attachment to and anxious care about such life affairs;
> —freedom that is even more revolutionary than the small and large revolutions we are always tempted to undertake as the advocates of these concerns;
> —freedom that is more revolutionary because its foundation is the new, transforming attachment to God's kingdom.

With challenging tasks and unfolding relationships looming large before us, it is with special timeliness that we listen to these words, "Take therefore no thought for the morrow: for the morrow shall take thought for the things of itself."

But even as we strive to hear and see from the perspective of Kingdom wisdom, we may well feel the need to confess that puzzlement remains.

And so we pray, "We believe, but, O God, help thou our unbelief!" Renew these assurances and orientations within us:

—The "heavenly Father knoweth that we have need of all these things;"

—"Seek ye first the kingdom of God and his righteousness, and all these things shall be added unto you."

Remind us that we are not asked to seek the way as though our grateful, our obedient, our freedom-filled response were strictly of our own doing. The way has come to us. We have but to arise and walk. Help us, O God, to walk in your path of peace and righteousness. Amen.

30
FAMILY RECREATION

Why I Believe in Fishing

Why do I believe in fishing? When you are dealing with such a personal passion, giving convincing reasons becomes difficult. For those who share the passion, reasons are unnecessary. For those who do not, reasons are not likely to be persuasive.

I can sense what the skeptics among you are thinking. You mean you sleep in tents for a week on that isolated lakeside? You get up each morning at five o'clock to start circling the shoreline, dew scarcely breaking through the shadows, cool mist penetrating even the warmest clothing? You endure mosquitoes that think "Off" means "on" and "Cutters" means "all-out attack"? You put up with the dampness that invades tent and sleeping bags, leaky boats, wet feet, nagging rain, and lack of plumbing deemed absolutely essential any other week of the year? Why?

Why indeed? Such questions drive us quickly to "just because" language. Or to situations in which language functions in "odd" ways.

In support of such passions language has to convey more than direct, literal information. It has to invite others into a similar commitment. What is required is testimony or strong preaching more than argument.

Why do I believe in fishing? Not simply as a food-gathering activity, although that remains essential when your week's menus call for fish once a day with no corner grocery stores nearby. More to the point, though, are values such as these:

—experiencing yourself and your family and friends in a very different environment, accompanied by different friends over the years;

—regaining your appreciation for the simple necessities of life: fresh and cool water, shelter, and food as you count cookies, pineapple slices, pieces of fish, even handfuls of Fritos!

—sensing your interdependence in a situation where each person's contributions are vital to the welfare of the total group;

—testing your endurance;

—getting in touch with the earth and the variety of creatures it supports;

—expanding the stories that become living, nurturing memories, stories that create mental pictures more vivid and motivating than the photographs taken by a camera, stories that are quite particular, yet that put you in touch with larger meanings:

. . . learning to pull together with other, youthful and inexperienced, paddlers if progress is to be made in boats that do not easily paddle;

. . . "moving on" in face of such inevitable setbacks as broken fishing rods, fish lost because of a break in the metal fish stringer or an attacking turtle, and leaky boots;

. . . discovering the interconnections between compassion and justice, and the ambiguities of interventions into the status quo out of the very finest motives.

Larger values and meanings are equally central to the fishing stories of Luke 5 and John 21.

In Luke 5 we read about the people crowding around Jesus to hear him preach. He is being pressed toward the very shoreline of the lake. Jesus sees two boats, now empty because the fishermen are washing their nets. Finally Jesus catches the attention of one of the fishermen—Simon Peter—and asks "him to pull out a little from the land." That gives him breathing room, while keeping him close enough to be heard as he teaches the people.

When he is finished speaking, he says to Simon, "Try casting your nets on that deeper side of the boat." Simon replies that they had fished all night with no success; still he obeys Jesus' command. Simon and his companions catch so many fish that their nets are breaking and their boats sinking! All of them—Simon Peter as well as James and

John, the sons of Zebeddee—are astonished. Jesus says, "Do not be afraid. Henceforth you will have even bigger catches, for you will be catching men and women."

The John 21 account follows Jesus' resurrection. This time Jesus again meets fishermen by the lake—Simon Peter, Thomas called the twin, Nathaniel of Cana in Galilee, James and John, and two other unnamed disciples. The fish are not biting. Jesus instructs them to try it on the right side of the boat. They catch so many that they can scarcely haul in the net.

Later Jesus offers to help them prepare breakfast. When Jesus gives them some fish to eat and breaks bread with them, the disciples recognize who he is and rejoice.

The Scriptures do not present such stories simply because of the larger meanings they evoke. There is no lack of interest in the literal, direct aspects of the accounts—fishing as a routine activity, lack of success in that venture, and the surprising reversal of their poor fishing through Jesus' intervention.

The Scriptures do not feature allegorical meanings that are only loosely connected with or even detached from actual events.

In the Luke 5 and John 21 stories and throughout the Scriptures there are rich interconnections between events and meanings that link us to God's eternal purpose made personal in Jesus Christ.

Outcomes are truly amazing when we obey Jesus even in the face of such instructions as "Try casting on that deeper side of the boat." "But, Master, we fished there all night and caught nothing!" Still they obeyed, and they caught so many fish that their boats began to sink!

Obedience to the clear commands of Jesus—that accent stands out sharply in these Luke 5 and John 21 accounts. To be a disciple is to obey, even when the command goes contrary to clear expectations. "But, Master, we fished there all night and caught nothing!"

Clearly the church heard these stories of the miraculous catch of fish—even as we do—against the background of Jesus' total life and ministry. How often the actual outcomes of the disciples' obedience are unexpected, even shocking! Jesus repeatedly tried to help his disciples understand his coming passion and resurrection triumph. Yet immediately following the Crucifixion, in their perplexity and discouragement they returned to their familiar routine. "Simon Peter said to them, 'I am going fishing.' They said to him 'We will go with you.'"

Expectancy easily wanes or gets misdirected, something easily understood by all who engage in the activity of fishing!

It is at those moments when the call to obey comes with jarring impact and amazing results!

"Cast your net on the other side of the boat, and you will catch fish!" "Why do you seek the living among the dead? Remember how he told you, while he was still in Galilee, that the Son of man must be delivered into the hands of sinful men, and be crucified, and on the third day rise" (Luke 24:5b, 6). Yes, the outcomes are amazing and truly revolutionary. Obedience requires that we look for glory not in either sword or crown, but in the cross, in servanthood, in true regard for the neighbor, in a liberating trust that god's gracious intent is not overcome by alien principalities and powers, not even by death itself!

Fish caught in the net of Christ—that is one of the dominant symbols on the north wall of the Bethany Seminary chapel. It is placed under one of the overhanging arms of the cross.

That symbol has become the seminary logo. It appears on letterheads, in catalogs, and in a wide array of our publications. It is a daily reminder that discipleship involves not only obedience but also aggressive outreach. In the midst of their amazement Jesus said to Peter, James, and John what he says to all of us. "Do not be afraid; henceforth you will make even bigger catches, for you will be catching men and women."

Being caught in the net of Christ means being set free to witness, to bring others to Christ who, in his resurrection glory, deserves our full obedience, our confidence, and our redirected expectancy.

This Christ, who even now is seated at God's right hand, is also never distant from such ordinary activities as food-gathering and sharing a meal together.

"Jesus said to them, 'Bring some of the fish you have just caught.' So Simon Peter went abroad and hauled the net ashore, full of large fish, a hundred and fifty of them; and although there were so many, the net was not torn. Jesus said to them, 'Come and have breakfast.' Now none of the disciples dared ask him, 'Who are you?' They knew it was the Lord."

Why do I believe in fishing? Just because it reminds me of the table of the Lord. We gather at that table, on the lakeside or in our homes, on city or country streets, at church conferences. We gather in the strength of God's own invitation and in the power of Jesus' death and resurrection. "Jesus came and took the bread and gave it to them, and so with the fish." So I, ministering in his name, extend this invitation: Let us be partakers of the promise of the heavenly food in grateful obedience, faithful witnessing, and joyful recognition. So none of us dare ask him, "Who are you?" We know it is the Lord!

We Have Heard for Ourselves

We thank you, O God, that the net of Christ is sturdy enough to hold, even though we continue to squirm and struggle to escape.

Grant that we may not become so preoccupied with the net itself that we fail to respond fittingly to the one whose net it is. We thank you, O God, that symbols have their way with us, energizing, questioning, stirring, and sometimes nudging us sharply. Grant that we may rejoice in their servant role, but do not let us confuse lesser witnesses for the true Lord and Master. Grant that we may be empowered to say with those who encountered Jesus before us, "We have heard for ourselves, and we know that this is indeed the Savior of the world." Amen.

31

GOOD FRIDAY AND EASTER

Living in the Light of God's Remembering

Good Friday and Easter are as closely bound together as the sorrow and joy we experience in life.

The dramatic events of Easter did not diminish the poignancy of Jesus' Good Friday cry of dereliction, "My God, my God, why have you forsaken me?" That cry was as agonized as the cry of anyone suffering not only physical pain but also extreme loneliness and abandonment. Even more so, for it came from God's own anointed, the One sent from God, the very One of whom, John's Gospel says, "In the beginning was the Word, and the Word was with God, and the Word was God" (John 1:1).

It was at the tomb of Jesus "on the first day of the week, at early dawn" (Luke 24:1a) that Mary Magdalene, Joanna, Mary the mother of James, and the other women heard that incredible, even fearsome question, "Why do you seek the living among the dead?" (Luke 24:5b). They had come fully expecting to minister to the lifeless body of the one in whose grave also lay their dashed dreams and hopes. No wonder they were perplexed by what they saw (the empty tomb) and by what they heard (the announcement that he had risen!). They were not asked to forget the troublesome events of Good Friday but to receive the good news of Easter as the sign of a promise fulfilled. They were urged to remember how Jesus had told them, "while he was still in Galilee, that the Son of Man must be delivered into the hands of sinful men, and be crucified, and on the third day rise. And they remembered his words, and returning from the tomb they told all this to the eleven and to all the rest" (Luke 24:6-9).

"Why do you seek the living among the dead?" That was the question that was heard and that demanded a response from the women at the tomb of Jesus on that first Easter morn. That is the question we also hear and to which we must respond. When the apostles first heard the report of the women returning from the tomb, the women's "words seemed to them an idle tale, and they did not believe them" (Luke 24:11). But eventually many shared the transforming conviction and transmitted to succeeding generations the fact that the light of Easter had faced the darkness of Good Friday and the "darkness has not overcome it" (John 1:5b). When that life-saving conviction is ours, too, then we sense how the Cross and Resurrection form such a dynamic unity. Then in all times and circumstances we anticipate that the gloom of night will give way to the brightness of the new day that centers in Christ's victory. Then we are free to remember the pain as well as the joy of life, for we know that Good Friday and Easter are both included in God's great faithfulness.

We have an annual Christmas party at Bethany Seminary. It is a campus-wide event involving students, faculty, staff, and their families.

During one of those occasions several years ago there were the usual Christmas stories and songs. Persons were invited to share some meaningful Christmas memories.

A spouse of one of our seniors told how she was one of a family of daughters—not the oldest, but the tallest. Hence, in their family and church dramatizations of the Christmas story, she always ended up being Joseph, never Mary, never the baby Jesus.

She remembered her pain, her frustration, even her anger at that. Why always Joseph? But now, some years later, it all seemed different somehow. Those early memories of family and church events had become for her meaningful and much beloved—even the memory of always being Joseph!

Then she looked around the seminary lounge—fireplace brightly aglow, Christmas candles wafting their aroma through the room, children wriggling on the floor—their faces aglow with eagerness and anticipation.

She noted that next year's Christmas party at Bethany would be different. Some would be absent, while new faces would be added.

She was sad at the prospect of the change.

She also was made glad by the thought that five years or more from now this particular Christmas party and other memories related to our experience as a Bethany extended family would be remembered with love and appreciation—joy would break through our sorrow.

I shall never forget her recollections and her anticipations. She helped me sense afresh how our times of being sad and of being glad intermingle.

She also caused me to think of the way the God of Good Friday and Easter holds things together in our behalf. There are moments when sorrow and tears seem all there is. But then, like a friend who "stands by" in such times of deep gloom, God holds our joy and our sense of well-being in safekeeping until we can once again claim them for ourselves.

No sorrow can ever befall us that Jesus, a man of sorrows and ac-quainted with grief, has not already known. Jesus wept upon receiving news of the death of Lazarus, a close friend. His tears fell copiously when he pondered the people's stiff-necked rebellion and bondage to alien principalities and powers. Yet Jesus also entered into the gaiety and laughter of a wedding feast in Cana of Galilee. He knew the delights of close friendships, the laughter and spontaneity of children, the beauty of God's earth, and the excitement of challenging tasks well done.

Because Jesus shared our humanity with its mixtures of sorrow and joy, and because Jesus was God's own Word who "became flesh and dwelt among us, full of grace and truth" (John 1:14a), we no longer need cringe and hide as though the darkness had really gained the upper hand. We may live in the light of God's own remembering. For the God who raised Jesus from the dead even now remembers all our todays from the vantage point of those tomorrows when we shall claim the joy that breaks through our sorrow.

And so by God's grace and in God's strength, may we be em-powered each moment to greet both Good Friday and Easter as a sign of God's promise fulfilled, to draw upon the joy and sense of well-being that God ever holds for us in safekeeping, and then to express our heartfelt gratitude in deeds of lively witness and loving service.

32
GRADUATION

"Learning the River"
While Appreciating Its Awesome Majesty

Old Times is one of the earlier writings of Mark Twain. In that work Twain draws upon his own experience of being initiated into the disciplines of piloting a Mississippi riverboat.

He is sure that no books, no school, no theory will suffice to equip a person for the task. Important competencies can be learned only if there is also a direct encounter with the river.

What the river pilot has to learn is nothing less than a new language, the language of the river. The pilot must read that language by day and by night, in summer and in winter, when skies are clear and when treacherous fog closes in, when heading upstream or downstream. If the pilot is to be effective, the river must become an open book that delivers up its most guarded secrets.

Twain portrays the sense of freedom and power "learning the river" conveys to the initiated pilot. But in acquiring the new competencies, you may lose something too. In his words, "Now when I had mastered the language of this water and had come to know every trifling feature that bordered the great river . . . I had made a valuable acquisition. But . . . I had lost something which could never be restored to me while I lived. All the grace, the beauty, the poetry had gone out of the majestic river."

By way of illustration he compares two ways of experiencing a sunset on the river.

As he might have enjoyed it in his preinitiated innocence:
—standing like one bewitched as the river turns to blood in evening's glow;
 —delighting in a solitary log floating by, black and awesome;
  —watching a long, slanting mark sparkle on the water;
   —seeing boughs on the edge of the forest that glow like a flame;
    —and tracks on the water that shine like silver.

And then, as he would have responded to the sunset after his initiation as a pilot, having learned the language of the river:
—watching the same scene dispassionately;
 —knowing that the colorful sky in the West suggests there will be a wind tomorrow;
  —that the log floating by means the river is rising, small thanks to the driftwood being carried along;
   —that the slanting marks on the water signal a treacherous reef being formed by the shifting currents;
    —and that the trails on the water mark still another place that is shoaling up dangerously.

What Twain uncovers is the tension between the spontaneous enjoyment of a sunset on the river and learned competencies for navigating the river that may result in losing a sense of the river's awesome majesty.

This tension haunted Twain throughout his literary efforts. Repeatedly the characters in his novels have to cope with it. Huck Finn's life is especially tension filled. In his pilgrimage, Huck faced
—the tension between the river that supports the raft and its occupants' journey toward freedom, and the river with snags

located "in the very best place he could have found to fish for steamboats";

—the tension between moments when life on the raft is almost idyllic, and moments when out of treacherous fog lunges a monstrous steamboat, big, scary, inexorable, smashing unfeelingly through the raft;

—the tension between times on the river when "the nice breeze springs up, and comes fanning you from over there, so cool and fresh, and sweet to smell on account of the woods and flowers," and times that are not that way "because they've left dead fish lying around, gars, and such, and they do get pretty rank";

—the tension between life on the raft marked by Huck's and Jim's deepening loyalty and friendship, and life on the riverbanks marked by feuding, lynching, slave-owning, and other forms of inhumanity.

Nothing less than Huck's growth as a free and responsible human being is at stake in all this. Even though he always stands poised to "light out for the territory ahead of the rest," he cannot escape his most formative relationships with his drunken abusive father, with Jim the runaway slave, with Widow Douglas and Miss Watson, with the Duke and the Dauphin, with Tom Sawyer, with the Shepherdsons and Grangerfords, and with the everpresent river that flows through Huck's development as an integrating metaphor and point of reference.

These tensions and relationships are Huck's very special curriculum. On this commencement day we can say that his "readiness for graduation" is determined by how he responds to "final examination" questions like these: Will he experience the river with the spontaneous but often ineffective enjoyment of the uninitiated? Will he acquire and utilize the more effective but often joyless competencies of a trained pilot? Or will his growing maturity enable him to respond in a still more integrated way: appreciating the sparkling trails on the water, yet knowing how to steer the vessel safely around the shoals they also signify to the trained eye?

At an even more fundamental level, will he continue to help Jim, the runaway slave, in his flight to freedom, and thus transgress the law-abiding respectability of his day? Will he send the letter he has already written, which even now he holds in his trembling hand, the letter that will return Jim to slavery, or will he tear it up—as he eventually does—and thus choose fraternal caring at the cost of social disapproval?

The curriculum of you who are graduating has differed in many ways from Huck's. But for you too, nothing less is at stake than your ongoing growth as free, responsible, compassionate, courageous, appreciative human beings. For you too, "readiness for graduation" is determined by your answers to "final examination" questions like these:

Has "learning the river" meant that something priceless has been lost? While learning the competencies necessary for life itself and for your respective vocations, have you retained the capacity for wonder, for caring, for appreciation, for the courage of your convictions?

Having learned new language skills, can you still marvel at the first meaning-laden words of a child?

Having learned that it is possible to travel to the moon, even to hit a golf ball on its barren surface, can you still enjoy a romantic stroll in the moonlight?

Having learned the chemical composition of a teardrop, can you still weep with those who weep and laugh to the point of tears with those who rejoice?

Having learned the natural conditions that produce a rainbow, can you still affirm the words of the hymn, "We trace the rainbow through the rain and know the promise is not vain that morn shall tearless be"?

Having learned about quasars, planets, galaxies, and constellations, can you still resonate to the sentiment of the childhood verse, "Twinkle, twinkle, little star, how I wonder what you are"?

Having learned how to apply disciplined historical research to the Scriptures, can you still make the simple, life-shaping affirmation, "Jesus loves me, this I know, for the Bible tells me so"?

Questions like these are not abstract. They have a practical urgency to them. Therefore, they cannot be answered abstractly. They call for our commitments, our actions, our very dispositions, and not merely our thoughts and intentions.

Nor are these questions addressed only to you graduates. They are addressed to all of us. Answering them takes a lifetime. Commencements are important markers and rest stops along the way that allow us to catch our breath for the journey still ahead.

Answering these questions is a very personal undertaking, but it does not occur in isolation. We draw upon rich legacies of example and inspiration. A "great cloud of witnesses" precedes us. We are surrounded by many who are engaged in "learning the river" while appreciating its awesome majesty.

Schools that also serve as communities of faith and learning aim to help us acquire vocationally useful skills and also to develop as persons who care, who serve, who believe. In such formative environments we are claimed by the vision and the possibility of becoming trained persons for whom "all the grace, the beauty, the poetry" has not "gone out of the majestic river." That vision and possibility has added content through the Judeo-Christian heritage that has been transmitted to succeeding generations of us. This heritage speaks of the knowledge that issues in mastery and control, but it also reminds us that there is a still higher wisdom that we receive with humility and response-stirring gratitude. The source of that wisdom is the God of Abraham and Sarah, Isaac and Jacob, the God of all creation, the God in whose hands the rivers and the lakes, all living creatures are held, the God in whom "all things hold together."

The poetry of Alfred Tennyson speaks of that higher wisdom this way:

> Knowledge is of things we see;
> And yet we trust it comes from thee,
> A beam in darkness: let it grow.
> Let knowledge grow from more to more,
> But more of reverence in us dwell;
> That mind and soul, according well,
> May make one music as before.

Knowledge "of the things we see" issues in the ability to do things, and it is fitting that it be so. If we were still traveling the Mississippi by riverboat, we would want competent pilots. In the *practice* of all vocations we expect persons to be competent and well trained.

And so, "let knowledge grow from more to more." That, however, is only one side of Tennyson's vision, which goes on to say, "but more of reverence in us dwell, that mind and soul, according well, may make one music as before."

When both reverence and knowledge increase for you and for those of us here to congratulate you, then we are "ready for graduation." That is the educational outcome most worthy of our single-minded quest. That is the "pearl of great price," the "kingdom of hope and promise," the "maturity" for which we may yearn with tiptoe expectancy.

Yet that outcome, we also confess, is finally achieved not by our most heroic efforts but by the workings of a grace whose wisdom and power are far greater than our own. In the strength of that transcendent grace we celebrate our commencements, we put down our markers, we catch our breath for the journey still before us. We proceed in the chastened yet confident hope that we shall indeed continue "learning the river while appreciating its awesome majesty." We proceed with the heartfelt prayer that "mind and soul, [head and heart, competence and compassion, ability and appreciation] may make one music as before."

—Adapted from an article in *Messenger*, May 1982

33
LENT

A Call to Discipleship

The season of Lent is a time for listening and responding to the call to discipleship. Renewed obedience to that call entails "following after" Jesus, just as it did when Jesus asked his earliest disciples to leave their nets and follow him.

As portrayed in the Gospels, Jesus is both the embodiment and the mediator of the radical and distinctive freedom that is received as a gift of grace by those who place God's kingdom first in their affections, their loyalty, and their specific actions. Not merely in his teachings but in his deeds and in his very person, Jesus confronted his close followers and others around him with the intrusive claim of God's kingdom. He displayed his own response to that claim through a remarkable freedom in relation to a number of very practical affairs and involvements. To illustrate without at all attempting to be inclusive, recall his posture toward society's preoccupations with possessions and fame.

In relation to possessions there is no hint that he gave much thought about such matters as retirement plans, social security benefits, or the size of his estate. By a series of definite acts, by example and by precept he declared that the kingdom of God dethrones the kingdom of mammon. When he was put to death on the cross, the only recorded estate settlement was the casting of lots for his garments by the soldiers on guard.

He summons his followers in every generation to a similar freedom from misplaced reliance upon possessions: " . . . if any one would sue you and take your coat, let him have your cloak as well" (Matthew 5:40). "Do not lay up for yourselves treasures on earth, where moth and rust consume and where thieves break in and steal" (Matthew 6:19). "No one can serve two masters; . . . You cannot serve God and mammon" (Matthew 6:24). "Therefore do not be anxious, saying, 'What shall we eat?' or 'What shall we drink?' or 'What shall we wear?'" (Matthew 6:31). All such actions point in the same direction—freedom from inappropriate attachment to possessions. That freedom is what follows from listening and responding to the persistent and life-changing claim of God's kingdom upon us.

Jesus also displayed this freedom in relation to ordinary conceptions of fame, social status, and importance. In fact, he reversed these conceptions in dramatic ways. True status is found not in lording it over but in serving others, not in a crown and scepter but in a basin and towel, not in a sword but in a cross and empty tomb. By deed as well as word he declared that the kingdom of God dethrones those things generally accepted as worthy of special recognition among us.

He summons his followers to a similar freedom from misplaced attachment to fame: "Blessed are you when others revile you and persecute you and utter all kinds of evil against you falsely on my account" (Matthew 5:11). "But if any one strikes you on the right cheek, turn . . . the other also" (Matthew 5:39). "But whoever would be great among you must be your servant, and whoever would be first among you must be your slave" (Matthew 20:26-27). What remains central in all this is the relationship to Jesus, who not only points toward but also supports a life of freedom from all kinds of idolatrous dependence on things that deserve at best only our secondary loyalty.

The freedom Jesus displayed, the freedom to which we are summoned as his followers, is even more revolutionary than the small and large revolutions we are always tempted to undertake out of our anxious concern about such things as possessions and fame. This freedom is more revolutionary because its foundation is more secure than our own strivings to "follow after" Jesus, to walk "in his steps," to imitate his "great example."

We are to seek first God's kingdom, but the "good news" of this Lenten season is that God's kingdom has first sought us. It is from the new positioning based on God's intervention in our behalf that our strivings have their place and their possibility.

The New Testament speaks in different ways about God's gracious kingdom initiatives that center in Jesus Christ.

One way is in 2 Corinthians 5:17-18: "Therefore, if any one is in Christ, that person is a new creature; the old has passed away, behold, the new has come. All this is from God, who through Christ reconciled us to himself and gave us the ministry of reconciliation."

The word "reconciliation" also means "exchange." So the foundation of the revolutionary freedom to which the "followers after Jesus" are summoned is God's "exchange" accomplished in Jesus Christ in our behalf.

Reconciliation as exchange—what a powerful image! Like the teacher speaking to the school child, God says:

"Let me sit where you sit, so your life becomes my concern and my life becomes yours."

"Let your temptations be mine and my victories yours."

"Let your anxiety about material things and social recognition be mine and my confidence and freedom be yours."

In Jesus Christ God experiences life "from our side," like a strong, compassionate, wise teacher who helps us move from the darkness of ignorance and lostness into the light, the hope, the joy, and the freedom of truth.

In Jesus Christ we have God's own living Word made flesh, spelled out into our hands, indeed, into our corporate humanity, God's own living Word exchanging places with us, penetrating our blindness and deafness, giving us the light, hope, joy, and freedom
—that comes to those who seek God's kingdom first,
—that empowers us to translate our discipleship into specific deeds of obedient service,
—that calms "our unwise confusion," and bids "our clamor cease,"
—that lets our "anxious hearts grow quiet, Like pools at evening still, till God's reflected heavens All our spirits fill" (Harry Emerson Fosdick, "O God, in Restless Living").

O God, may this Lenten season be a time of renewed obedience for all of us. Empower us to "follow after" Jesus so we may show forth our gratitude for your reconciling love and carry on your ministry of reconciliation, which is the light, the hope, the joy, and the freedom of our discipleship. Amen.

34

LOVE FEAST

Opening Words

We come to this table in the strength of God's own invitation made personal in Jesus Christ. "Behold, I stand at the door and knock; if any one hears my voice and opens the door, I will come in to him, and will eat with him, and he with me" (Revelation 3:20). "Ask, and it will be given: seek, and you will find; knock, and it will be opened to you" (Matthew 7:7; Luke 11:9).

We come to this table with confidence, for the love that taber-
nacled among us in Jesus Christ has survived death and the grave. We
stand in the faith of the early followers of this man from Galilee, who
testified to his victory and continued presence. One such follower
gave us this shared affirmation: "Who shall separate us from the love
of Christ? Shall tribulation, or anguish, or persecution, or famine, or
nakedness, or peril, or sword? . . . No, in all these things we are more
than conquerors through him who loved us. For I am sure that neither
death, nor life, nor angels, nor principalities, nor things present, nor
things to come, nor powers, nor height, nor depth, nor anything else
in all creation, will be able to separate us from the love of God in
Christ Jesus our Lord" (Romans 8:35, 37-39).

We come to this table with gladness, for we are assured that the
forgiveness that was incarnate in Jesus Christ is made perfect in
weakness. We have been invited not because of high position,
superior virtue, or a job well cone. We have not been gathered
because we deserve some type of meritorious service award. We are
here because Jesus cared enough for his neighbors to follow his convictions to the cross. Since he tied no strings to his love, we need make
no claim to merit but may lean upon his prior activity on our behalf.

The Feet Washing

We are here at the invitation of God, in confidence and gladness.
These clear instructions are given to those who would follow after
Jesus. "If I your Lord and master have washed your feet, you ought to
wash one another's feet." By our presence at this table we indicate our
desire to be numbered among the disciples. And so we obey the command. We wash one another's feet. In some ways the reason for this
part of our service is as simple as that. It is an act of obedience.

This service also acts out our willingness to serve and to be served.
There is something intrinsically good about compassionate aid to a
brother or sister in need. The basin and towel offered to us by the
neighbor also speaks of our willingness to be served. We commit
ourselves to the neighbor in such a way that we seek that person's
total well-being and welcome that person's ability to serve us.

It acts out our intention to remain faithful to and be renewed in
our baptismal vows. The Lord's Supper presupposes baptism. Feet
washing calls to mind that prior commitment. Baptism is more than an
abstract religious rite. It is at the same time a profound social reality. For
baptism is the ordinance of the unity among persons wrought by God
in overcoming the power and reign of death, in overcoming, that is,
all that alienates, segregates, divides and destroys persons in their relations to each other, within their own persons, and in their relation-

ships with the rest of creation.

As we gird ourselves with towels and kneel to wash one another's feet, may these understandings become our conviction and our life commitment.

Scripture: John 13:1-18

Hymn: "Teach Me, O Lord, Thy Holy Way"

The Love Feast

This meal links us to an upper room in ancient Palestine. Jesus gathered his associates for a time of closeness and sharing in the face of an uncertain future. He had so completely pursued his vision of God's kingdom of righteousness and peace that he was now facing the wrath of his enemies. He knew that his death was imminent.

Because Jesus in far-off Palestine lived and died for others, this commemorative meal also links us with the coming of God's kingdom purpose into our lives today. We recognize that kingdom's presence whenever there is true regard for the neighbor's welfare, whenever there is caring, integrity and trust, whenever community emerges that no longer divides on the basis of color, creed, social status, or any other artificial barrier, whenever one faces another in openness and honesty.

Because that kingdom reality is still blurred in our midst due to human frailty and sin, this meal also points ahead to that "end time" when we shall participate in the messianic banquet, when what is now only provisionally realized in our community reaches its fulfillment.

We sit together at this meal as children in God's household. We eat together in thankfulness, in recollection of the Upper Room, and in anticipation of the marriage supper of the Lamb of God. Let us hear the Scripture lesson as we reflect further upon that love that is made manifest in the sharing of God's good gift of food.

Scripture: John 15:1-15

Prayer for the Meal

O God, we thank you for the love that has claimed us in Jesus Christ, the love that cares first and asks questions second, the love that breaks through self-preoccupations to genuine regard for the neighbor, the love that reaches toward the brother or sister with a helping hand rather than a clenched fist, the love that suffers death on a cross on behalf of righteousness and peace.

We confess that our capacity to love falls short of Christ's claim upon us. Callousness strives against caring. Concern for self gets in the way of openness to the neighbor. We prefer to dominate rather than to serve. We shrink from suffering for righteousness' sake. We should like to pretend that it is not so, but we know that we fall short of our own highest aspirations.

We rejoice that the love of Christ genuinely and freely reaches toward us. Otherwise we could not gather at this table at all. Revive within us the willingness to have Christ's Spirit direct our lives. We are grateful that this meal of love participates in that "end time" when we shall share in the messianic banquet, when what is already provisionally realized in our community reaches its fulfillment. We eat together in thankfulness, in glad anticipation of the marriage supper of the Lamb of God. We eat together as a sign of our desire to participate in Christ's love. We seek cleansing and strengthening of our faith and discipleship. Receive our prayer and our activities in the name and Spirit of Christ. Amen.

Let us partake of the meal in joy and glad anticipation.

Celebrating Christ's Presence

The Lord who wears a victor's crown is the same Lord who in his humility took a basin and towel and symbolically washed the feet of all humanity. The Lord who in his eternal reign bears the "marks of slaughter upon him" is the same Lord whose "real presence" is to be sought and obeyed wherever people long for the freedom of the children of God. We celebrate Christ's presence in the breaking of bread and the drinking of the cup because we know he is present wherever men and women cry out for justice and mercy. In partaking of the bread and cup we affirm our faith that God's purpose is on the side of those who suffer the cross rather than sanction inhumanity to persons, on the side of those who stand for the right even when it is unpopular, on the side of those who place service ahead of status, love ahead of power, justice ahead of personal privilege, humility before God ahead of pride in the sight of other men and women.

Scripture: Isaiah 53:1-12

Hymn: "Christ, We Do All Adore Thee"

The Bread

Words of Institution: For I have received from the Lord that which I also delivered unto you, that the Lord Jesus the same night in which he was betrayed took bread and when he had given thanks, he broke it, and said, "Take, eat. This is my body, which is broken for you. This do in remembrance of me."

So I, ministering in his name, take bread and ask God's blessing upon it. Let us pray.

O God, we thank you for a piece of bread. It speaks to us of earth: the soil, the sun, the rain, the air have cooperated in its formation.

It speaks to us of persons: human toil, technical skill, loving care have contributed to its present shape.

It speaks to us of heaven; your purpose has been implanted in the commonplace things and events of life—the eating of a meal, the performance of a menial but needy service, the eager clamorings of children, the explosive vigor of youth, and the quiet serenity of the aging.

We thank you that this bread is already blessed by your loving providence, and especially by Jesus who taught us that your Spirit is as close as the food we eat and the air we breathe. Strengthen us for your kingdom purpose as we receive this gift of life. In the name of One who died for his conviction that divine holiness tabernacles even in so simple an act as the eating of bread in openness to the neighbor, even Christ our Lord. Amen.

Unison (each person breaking bread with a neighbor): This bread that we share is the communion of the body of Christ.

Let us eat of this bread in joy and glad anticipation.

The Cup

Words of Institution: On the same night of betrayal, he took a cup, and when he had given thanks, he gave it to them, saying "Drink of it, all of you; for this is my blood of the covenant which is poured out for many for the forgiveness of sins."

So I, ministering in his name, take the cup and ask God to bless it. Let us pray.

O God, bless this cup. We are grateful for the nurturing images that surround it: Jesus praying in the garden that he might be spared the cup of his agony only to affirm "Not my will but yours be done"; Jesus facing into the loneliness of standing in our human alienation, "My God, my God, why have you forsaken me?"; Jesus' life and ministry celebrated by his followers as the cup of the new covenant. In drinking from this cup we share that vision of a kingdom of righteousness and peace that was foreshadowed in Jesus. Grant us the grace to live in eager anticipation of that kingdom, rejoicing in its presence whenever there is true regard for our neighbor's welfare. Bless this cup as an instrument for the renewal of our discipleship. Hear our prayer in the name and Spirit of Christ. Amen.

Unison: This cup that we share is the communion of the blood of Christ.

Let us drink the cup in joy and glad anticipation.

Prayer

O God, now that we have shared in the feet washing, the meal, the bread, and the cup, grant that we shall share afresh in Christ's humility and love, in Christ's obedience and faith, in Christ's trust and hope. Inspire us to carry into the everydayness of our lives all to which we aspire when your presence is most deeply felt. May our faith and hope have feet and hands, a voice and a heart, so that we may serve and witness to the "good news" in Jesus Christ. We offer our prayers and our committed lives in the name of the One who is the "way, the truth, and the life." Amen.

Hymn: "O, Master, Let Me Walk With Thee"

Benediction: "The grace of the Lord Jesus Christ, the love of God the Father, and the communion of the Holy Spirit be with you all." Amen.

35
MARRIAGE
Tied and Tangled in Life's Promise

L ife weaves a fabric of promises around us. It is a thing of great beauty like a coat of many colors, like a spider web quivering in the sunlight, like a rainbow spanning the heavens.

We become not only tied but tangled in life's promises. There is no escaping these entanglements. Nor would we want to! Human relationships based on fidelity and love are among our deepest, most lasting satisfactions.

The making and keeping of promises takes us to the very heart of the Scriptures. It is a God-like quality.

In Genesis it is presented as part of being created in the "image of God." "So God created him; male and female he created them."

Man and woman are cocreated. The Genesis account pictures this as a fact of delight and joy! Recall the scene. When the eyes of the man, who had been helping God name the creatures, light upon the female of his own species, he said, "This at last is bone of my bones and flesh of my flesh; she shall be called woman . . . ."

The Hebrew language is even stronger, something like, "Wow! Lord, you really did it this time!"

Created in the image of God—made for relationships, for a life of mutuality and shared commitment, made to be promise makers and keepers like God!

God sets the pattern, provides the model for the human relationships we are to "image." God relates to creation

—in love, reaching out without waiting for persons to earn approval—breaking through closed circles to include the wayfarers, the neglected and forgotten ones;
—in faithfulness, with steadfastness and reliability in covenant, with an aggressive righteousness that enables what it demands;
—in trustworthiness, tied to and tangled with creation so completely that God suffers in Christ so that the promise might be established in face even of the strongest enemy!

You are created in the "image of God" to be partners in the ongoing work of creation—to name one another, and thus to give each other strength and joy: "Wow, Lord, you did it this time!" You are called to be promise keepers like God!

Let your life together be marked by

—care: deep, genuine, unspoiled by neglect and indifference. Know that your caring for one another has its foundation in God's own love.
—integrity: steady, reliable, unshaken by deceit and betrayal. Know that your fidelity has its security in God's prior faithfulness.
—trust: clear, firm, unspoiled by suspicion. Know that your trust has its grounding in God's own trustworthiness.

For a Life of True Caring and Service

Thank you, O God, for the joys of life, for the beauty of persons in love, for the firm ties of friendship, for special gatherings and times of high celebration.

We pray especially for _____ and _____ . Strengthen them for the life of true caring and service to which they so sincerely aspire.

Be to them a source of unfailing confidence in the face of discouragement. Let them experience the thrill of lives well spent as obedient followers of Christ. Give them the single-minded devotion to seek first your kingdom and your righteousness so that their love for one another might be an inspiration to others.

Be pleased to bless all those who have assembled here this day to share in the promises _____ and _____ have made to each other as part of their marriage covenant. Renew within us the vision of your faithfulness and outgoing love as the only firm foundation for a life of true regard for one another. In Christ's name. Amen.

36

MEMORIAL SERVICE

Opening Words and Prayer

We gather in grateful remembrance and celebration. We represent the community of faith from which our sister has drawn strength, the community that continues to be strengthened by her witness, the community in which she received her early glimpses of the resurrection life that is now hers. We bring all our deepest feelings and needs to this service: our bafflement, our grief, our anger, our memories, our commitments and anticipations. Let us pray.

We are grateful, O God, for the ties that bind our hearts in Christian love: for your own "immortal love, forever full, forever flowing free," poured into our hearts through Christ.

To all members of the family, to all of us who share the loss death brings, grant, we pray, a renewed sense of being members of one another, held firm by cords of compassion and ropes of love that nothing in all creation can ever tear apart. Through Christ, the source of our life and of the hope that endures. Amen.

God's Yes on All His Promises

2 Corinthians 1:1-2; 18-22

The Apostle Paul reminds the Corinthians in one of his letters to them of God's faithfulness and of the straight dealings that he and his

companions have had with them in the past. In all of their relationships with the Corinthians, Silvanus, Timothy, and Paul had not
vacillated, saying Yes and No at once. "For the Son of God, Jesus
Christ, whom we preached among you was not Yes and No, but in
him it is always Yes. For all the promises of God find their Yes in him"
(2 Corinthians 1:19-20a).

Jesus Christ is God's Yes to all his promises. That affirmation brings
us to the very heart of the gospel, the "good news" that sustains and
quickens us even in our moments of deepest need.

God's promise that "he shall be our God, and we shall be his people"
(Lev. 26:12) shines like a beacon throughout the Scriptures.

That promise is renewed with freshness and great power
throughout God's dealings with the creation.

We see God's promise in the portrait of God the Shepherd who
leads us beside still waters, who restores our souls, who leads us in
paths of righteousness for his name's sake, who walks with us through
the valley of the shadow of death so we fear no evil; whose rod and
staff comfort us, who makes certain that goodness and mercy shall
follow us all the days of our life, and we will dwell in the house of the
Lord forever (Psalm 23).

We see God's promise in Isaiah's vision that "even youths shall
faint and be weary, and the young shall fall exhausted; but they who
wait for the Lord shall renew their strength, they shall mount up with
wings like eagles, they shall run and not be weary, they shall walk and
not faint" (Isaiah 40:30-31).

We see God's promise in Jesus facing Satan in the wilderness, being
tempted in our place and in our behalf, moving aggressively into that
ambiguous realm in which Satan's power and God's's will become confused, steadfastly facing the most formidable enemy of God's promise, and remaining obedient to his mission as God's anointed.

We see God's promise in Jesus enduring death on the cross as the
One "who was despised and rejected," who "has borne our griefs and
carried our sorrows," who "was wounded for our transgressions" and
"bruised for our iniquities," and with whose "stripes we are healed"
(Isaiah 53:3-5).

We see God's promise in the assurance that Jesus, even now in his
resurrection glory, is seated at the right hand of the Father interceding
for us, and in his words of great comfort: "Let not your hearts be
troubled; believe in God, believe also in me. In my Father's house are
many rooms; if it were not so, would I have told you that I go to
prepare a place for you? And when I go and prepare a place for you, I
will come again and will take you to myself, that where I am you may
be also" (John 14:1-4).

Jesus Christ is God's unwavering Yes to the promise that "he shall be our God, and we shall be his people," God's covenant family, Christ's own resurrection body.

I believe firmly that our sister lived at the very center and in the strength of God's promise. She bore witness to that centeredness in quiet yet forceful ways: in her dedicated teaching, in her devotion to family and a wide circle of friends who felt and returned her love, in her willingness to serve her church by singing in the choir, serving in support of fellowship activities, working in church school.

I believe that she is equally secure and centered this moment in the steadfastness of God's promise. For that promise is more certain than the rising and setting of the sun, more reliable than the rotation of the earth on its axis, more predictable than the changing of the seasons. For in God's eternal promise "an age is but a day, and God watches sun give place to sun and planets burn away."

Renewed now by that same promise, may the God of redeeming and suffering love continue to be to us a friend of friends whose concern is never more than a whisper away. May we be granted courage to face the future with restored confidence, a confidence whose foreshadowings have already been established in Jesus Christ, a confidence that helps us greet our tomorrows with deepened joy and readiness to build new worlds in Christ's name. May we be given a clearer sense of membership in "Christ's body"—for in that body, that covenant family of God, we have our wholeness and our security, we have our strength and victory, Christ has conquered every enemy of God's promise—even death itself. In that body, that household of faith, we know a peace that passes all understanding—we know that morn shall tearless be. Amen.

37

ORDINATION

Ministry: Our Calling to Fulfill

The Christian ministry is a unique calling, not quite like any other, in spite of parallels with other disciplined efforts.

Ministry requires the empowerment of the Spirit to give it both faithfulness and effectiveness. "And his gifts were that some should be apostles, some prophets, some evangelists, some pastors and teachers" (Ephesians 4:11). The accent falls upon the Spirit's gifts, not upon the persons receiving and expressing those gifts.

The gifts of ministry are varied: apostolic, prophetic, evangelistic, pastoral, educational—yet they are sharply focused. All gifts of ministry are aimed toward the equipment of "the saints for the work of ministry, for building up the body of Christ" (Ephesians 4:12). That is their goal. Then these more specific objectives are added. Their obedient service is to help all "attain to the unity of the faith and of the knowledge of the Son of God, to maturity, to the measure of the stature of the fulness of Christ" (Ephesians 4:13).

In language less directly related to the text, we can add such qualities of the "equipped" person as these:

—commitment to life-long learning;

—service out of a deep sense of calling;

—freedom from self-centered preoccupations and needs;

—clarity and forcefulness in expressing your deepest convictions;

—the ability to adapt your knowledge and skills in varied relationships and circumstances;

—the capacity to stand with others in times of special need;

—the willingness to be disciplined by the same community within which you are commissioned to serve;

—respect for the heritage that shapes contemporary life while creatively remaining open to new insights and directions.

Through wisdom greater than our own, ministry utilizes such qualities. But the Scriptures remind us forcefully that all acquired knowledge and skills need to be enlivened by other markings that have even greater priority. We should all, for example, most "earnestly desire" the "higher gifts" of faith, hope, and love.

For truly, if we speak in the tongues of human beings and of angels, but have not love, we are noisy gongs and clanging symbols. If we have prophetic powers, understand all mysteries and all knowledge, if we have all faith so as to move mountains, if we complete an academic program with highest honors, but have not love, we fall far short of excellence in ministry. If we have not love, we are not "equipped for the work of ministry, for building up the body of Christ."

Because it is such a lofty calling, ministry presents us with some distinctive and most deadly temptations.

Sydney J. Harris, writing for the *Chicago Sun Times*, helps us identify one such temptation. He describes watching a performance of the play "Amadeus," about the intertwined lives of Mozart and his fellow composer Salieri:

> It was an interesting and often moving production, with a finely crafted script and for the most part excellent acting, although perhaps a touch overdirected. But the evening as a whole was a delight—at least to nonprofessional ears and eyes.

After the play, however, I had a cup of coffee with an old acquaintance who has long been an actor and director and drama coach. He admired some aspects of the production but found far more in it to criticize.

I am sure that his criticism was just and his judgments more perspicacious than mine—but the point is that his intimate knowledge of the mechanics of stagecraft and his awareness of nuances and subtleties both contributed to his enjoyment and at the same time limited his spontaneous reaction to the play.

He saw more than I did, but it was almost like examining a beautiful woman's skin under a microscope, and observing only the enlarged pores rather than noting the creamy complexion. Or, to change the metaphor, he was so aware of the peeling bark on the trees that he neglected the beauty of the forest.

In ministering we too may lose the capacity for spontaneity, for enjoyment, and for deep appreciation. In terms appropriate to our calling, we may also become "so aware of the peeling bark on the trees that we neglect the beauty of the forest." Disciplines of the mind may run ahead of disciplines of the soul. In gaining new levels of competence we may be less able to respond with compassion. In the graphic language of Sydney Harris, "seeing too much is as fatal as seeing too little, whether in a masquerade, a mosaic, or a mate"—and, we may add, in all aspects of our ministering as well.

Karl Barth helps us identify another of the temptations that so easily overtakes us. He gave the following admonitions to a group of ministers gathered in a retreat setting to hear him expound on the Apostles' Creed according to the Heidelberg Catechism, and Calvin's commentary on both:

The Heidelberg Catechism (34) says on this matter: "Wherefore callest thou him, our Lord?—Because he hath redeemed us, both soul and body, from all our sins, not with gold or silver, but with his precious blood, and hath delivered us from all the power of the devil; and thus made us his own property." . . . He not only was established by his Father to the end of having us under his governance. But he did something to be our Lord, and he is our Lord in doing it. We are his property because he has redeemed us, because he has acquired us for himself through his blood, that is, with his life. Therefore, he is our Lord in that he is our Savior.

Our Lord. No compartment of our existence is withdrawn from that Lordship. . . .

It is very important to stress this *"our* Lord." For we might have understood all about Christology and gone back home to start a general renewal of our lives and our churches to the unanimous admiration of the world. And yet Jesus Christ would not be our Lord, but we would be the lords of Jesus Christ. You all know, I think, this to be the last seduction, the last spiritual peril. We have understood, we are happy, we grasp, we grasp him instead of letting him grasp us, instead of submitting ourselves, instead of obeying. We change the Lord into a human entity of superior order, to be sure, very superior; . . . and at bottom, that is why we are so unhappy. There we are always with our little Christianities, with various brands of it. We are his advocates instead of his being our Advocate. We intercede for him instead of letting him intercede. We suffer (oh yes! we suffer) but then what about Christ's sufferings? And we are even resurrected; but now a very refined reversal takes place, a very dangerous one with which we delude ourselves concerning our "new lease on life." It is very important that we should reverse everything and learn how to say truly: our Lord, not I, but he, the Lord. And to learn how to live within this continuous quest, the quest of him who loves me and leads me (Karl Barth, *The Faith of the Church*, pp. 75-76).

"Ministry: Our Calling to Fulfill!" A unique calling. Requiring the gifts and empowerment of the Spirit. Fraught with some distinctive and most deadly temptations.

And so we make this confession with both humility and expectancy: ministry may draw strength from sound training, high intelligence, and acquired competencies, but only as mind and soul, head and heart, competence and compassion, ability and appreciation continue to "make one music as before." In ministry we till the soil, we plant and water, we cultivate and harvest, but it is God who gives the increase. "The work is thine, O Christ, the cause for which we stand. And being thine, "twill overcome its foes on every hand." We may thank God that it is so!

For Those Called to Set-Apart Ministry

Almighty God, we are grateful for the calling to ministry that these persons set apart today have received and accepted; for the depth of their commitment to that ministry; for the gifts of the Spirit with which they have been endowed; for the families, congregations, and districts that have contributed to their spiritual formation.

Help them to sense the support of the church through this act of commissioning, the church's invitation to them to serve in the full strength of their call and the spirit's enabling power.

In the days and years of service that lie ahead, help them to rekindle your gift that is within them through the laying on of hands. Take away any excessive pride and any excessive reticence in leadership.

Give them the spirit of power and love and self-control. Through their commissioning to special service, grant that the larger church shall be recommissioned in its shared ministry. Through Christ our Lord we pray. Amen.

38
PENTECOST

Where the Spirit Is!

The understanding we have of the nature of the church and its calling is shaped by some weighty New Testament images.

Think of 1 Corinthians 12:12-13: "For just as the body is one and has many members, and all the members of the body, though many, are one body, so it is with Christ. For by one Spirit we were all baptized into one body—Jews or Greeks, slaves or free—and all were made to drink of one Spirit."

Subsequent verses in the chapter expand the image by reminding us that a body is made up of many parts but still functions as a unit. The parts do not cease to be parts of the body even if they seek to withdraw because of envy or rebellion. Each part is vital for the total health of the body. The weakest parts seem to warrant more consideration. If one part hurts, all hurt, and if one is given special honor, all are honored.

And then this conclusion: "Now you are the body of Christ and individually members of it" (1 Corinthians 12:27). And each member brings distinctive gifts for the upbuilding of Christ's body.

Think also of Ephesians 2:19-22, where several images are presented in striking combination:

> So then you are no longer strangers and sojourners, but you are fellow citizens, with the saints and members of the household of God, built upon the foundation of the apostles and prophets, Christ Jesus himself being the chief cornerstone, in whom the whole structure is joined together and grows into a holy temple in the Lord; in whom you also are built into it for a dwelling place of God in the Spirit" (Ephesians 2:19-22).

Notice how the cornerstone image is linked with household and a type of bodily growth.

"Cornerstone" in this passage is used in a surprising way. It is not a foundation stone. The apostles and prophets serve that function. Rather it is a stone completing the uppermost angle of a gable roof, the very top of the building, the stone that points the direction and gives perfection to the whole building.

The imagery is fluid, imaginative, directional. In Christ, the uppermost stone, the whole structure is joined together and grows into a holy temple in the Lord. The structure keeps expanding, for we too are to be "built into it for a dwelling place of God in the Spirit."

Body—household—cornerstone—temple: It is the Spirit of the crucified-risen Christ who holds these images together and who is the source of the church's continuing life and service.

For where the Spirit is, there persons are empowered to "grow up in every way into him who is the head, into Christ, from whom the whole body, joined and knit together by every joint with which it is supplied, when each part is working properly, makes bodily growth and upbuilds itself in love" (Ephesians 4:15a-16).

Where the Spirit is, there persons are becoming part of the living structure of which Christ is chief cornerstone, growing into a "holy temple in the Lord," being "built into it for a dwelling place of God in the Spirit."

Where the Spirit is, there the church as Christ's crucified-resurrected body is visible today, even as it was on that first day of Pentecost when people from quite different cultural backgrounds, people who spoke in their own distinctive languages, could nevertheless understand each other telling "the mighty works of God" (Acts. 2:11b).

Where the Spirit is, there is the miracle of a unity among persons and groups that centers not in congeniality and like-mindednes, not even in our most earnest efforts to achieve it, but in the gracious gift of freedom to lead a life worthy of our calling as followers after Jesus, "with patience, forebearing one another in love, eager to maintain the unity of the Spirit in the bond of peace" (Ephesians 4:2-3).

Where the Spirit is, there is humble confession that there "are varieties of gifts, but the same Spirit; there are varieties of service but the same Lord; there are varieties of working; but it is the same God who inspires them all in everyone. To each is given the manifestation of the Spirit for the common good" (1 Corinthians 12:5-7).

Where the Spirit is, there is "eagerness for the Spirit's manifestations," and there is the will to "excel in building up the church" (1 Corinthians 14:12).

And so, by God's grace, let us live as befits those who are indeed disciples of Jesus Christ, who were "sealed with the promised Holy Spirit, who is the guarantee of our inheritance until we acquire possession of it, to the praise of his glory" (Ephesians 1:13b-14).

39

TIMES OF PATRIOTIC FERVOR
The Church and the American Dream

A Personal Faith Statement

The church is called and empowered
—to set out as a pilgrim people on a journey of faith and
obedience;
—to guard the dignity and rights of others, the distant neighbor
and the one close at hand, the enemy as well as the friend;
—to care for strangers and sojourners, remembering that all
members of God's household are members by God's grace
alone;
—to draw strength from the varied gifts of the Spirit;
—to commission and be commissioned in support of leaders who
lead and who help equip the whole people for the work of
ministry, of service;
—to share the faith dynamically, affirming by life and deed that
it is Jesus who leads us in our faith and brings it to perfection.

This paragraph is a personal faith statement. This vision of the
church claims my energies and judges my disobedience and lack of
courage. I also believe that it is a shared vision, one that claims all of
us, a vision that inspires and directs our energies.

The worldwide church lives and serves in particular cultures.
Such cultures offer both opportunities for and challenges to faith
development and sharing. How that is so should become clearer as we
explore our theme, "The Church and the American Dream."

The American Dream

References to the American dream recur as part of our cultural
self-understanding. When running for his first term of service, President Reagan evoked it as a way of encouraging campaign support for
Republican candidates. He linked qualities like these to the American
dream: family, productivity, initiative, patriotism, opportunity. As his
term progressed, he urged "staying on course," continuing the path of
supply-side economics and other features of his platform that he
repeatedly described as "a new beginning for the nation," a chance to
"start over" after the failures of previous administrations.

Beginning again, opportunity for a new and better life—these are
dominant notes in the American dream, and Ronald Reagan is not the
first President to appeal to the power of that pervasive vision.

The American dream is really a multifaceted, complex, developing vision that intermingles with the American church's calling to be the church in this particular cultural setting.

To catch varied glimpses of the American dream, I propose to help us remember some fictional and real-life personalities who especially typify and give shape to our collective American experience.

Huckleberry Finn

He is one of literature's "good-bad" boys.

He lacks any deep, sustaining family roots, His drunken father is his only close blood relative. Rather than coming from a nurturing home, he is always seeking a home.

He is addicted to truth. He cannot lie to himself, although he can spin out to someone else one yarn after another, quickly and with great ingenuity. The runaway slave, Jim, was with Huck on the raft when his pursuers were about to recapture him. Huck deterred them with a story about smallpox on the raft. At other times, he invented make-believe personal identities, as when he went ashore to get information that might help Jim continue his escape. Huck dressed as a little girl and almost succeeded with his disguise until the observant woman he was questioning noticed that Huck caught the spool of thread she tossed to him not like a girl but like a boy.

He is spontaneously compassionate. At a circus others took delight in a drunken clown trying to ride a horse. Huck exclaims, "It wasn't funny to me. I was all a-tremble to see his danger." When con artists Duke and King are caught, tarred, and feathered, Huck was pained. "I was sorry for them poor pitiful rascals. Human beings can be awful cruel to one another."

He draws moral insight and spiritual strength from nature. The river forms a contrast to life in settlements along its shoreline. The river has its own treacherous fogs and shifting currents, but gives Huck a vantage point for seeing and commenting on the acts of inhumanity only humans inflict on others.

He senses that society threatens to intrude upon life on the river. Those pursuing Jim, the runaway slave, are relentless in their efforts to recapture him. One day a riverboat looms suddenly out of the fog, its paddle wheel churning a song of death and destruction, and smashes unfeelingly into their raft.

He shares society's limited views. He sometimes speaks of Jim as "his property." He struggles with his conscience about helping Jim.

Eventually he breaks with social norms. He writes a letter informing on Jim. But he remembers Jim as a friend, not as a slave. He tears up the letter after intense struggle, willing to accept society's condemnation.

He remains restless and poised, ready to "light out for the territory ahead of the rest!" As he says it: "Aunt Sally she's going to adopt me and civilize me, and I can't stand it. I been there before!"

John Wayne (his TV and movie personality)

He had great strength and resourcefulness.

He was oriented toward the boundless, unexplored frontier with its freedom, danger, and challenge.

He did not easily conform to social routines and expectations.

He was capable of compassion toward those in need, and also of great anger—even violence—toward those committing acts of injustice.

He was brash, even vulgar and disdainful, when confronted by society's shallowness and phoniness.

In many ways he is remembered as a "representative American hero:" self-reliant, self-motivated, confident in his own unique and inner resources, a rugged, free-standing individual, compassionate but always strong, resourceful, usually at the edge of social relationships and commitments—he rarely kissed, let alone married, the heroine.

Abraham Lincoln

Recall that President Reagan listed "opportunity" and "patriotism" among qualities of the American dream.

Abe Lincoln uniquely typified these traits. From humble origins he struggled upward, and by great perserverance reached the highest office, from log cabin to White House. With great reluctance he accepted the call to leadership, and even with forebodings about possible death he served his country at a critical time, giving his life as a sacrifice to help save the Union.

He embodied "wilderness virtues:" guilelessness, honesty, endurance, straight speech, earthiness, lack of social pretentiousness, truthfulness, reluctant but courgeous performance of necessary tasks in behalf of others, even in the face of extreme danger.

Martin Luther King, Jr.

Nearly all of us have direct memories of this man and have personally felt his impact. How would you measure the influence of his life, his preaching, his leadership, his death? He dramatically affected the way all of us now experience the American dream.

His "I have a Dream!" speech still speaks for many, and with great power.

He voiced the anger of those who found no upward mobility in society through hard work and struggle, those for whom the promise of a better life seemed hollow, somehow for others but not for them.

He emerged as a living challenge to those who are enjoying the social benefits of the promise to include those now excluded, for they also are to receive the rights and dignity that justice requires.

He redefined patriotism. His persistence on a nonviolent path of active resistence, even to the point of his death, was for love of country, but not for country as it is but as it can become only when "justice rolls down like waters, and righteousness as an everflowing stream."

The American dream has from the earliest beginnings included biblical imagery. Our nation in its infancy was often likened to Israel's Exodus (leaving Europe), moving through the Red Sea (crossing the Atlantic), entering the Promised Land (the new country of virgin soil and boundless expanse), with a mission to be a "light to the nations" (the American experiment as a new venture in freedom and government "by the people"). Early there was a search for a United States seal. Jefferson proposed one with the children of Israel being led by a cloud by day and a pillar of fire by night. Franklin advocated one in which Moses was lifting up his wand dividing the Red Sea while Pharoah was being overwhelmed by its rushing waters.

Martin Luther King evoked biblical imagery in his preaching and in his persistence even unto death. He sounded a prophetic note. For this country to be a new Israel, a light to the nations, we must understand our calling not in terms of God's favor and privilege but in terms of being subject to God's sovereign reign. "And what does the Lord require of you, but to do justice, and to love kindness, and to walk humbly with your God?" (Micah 6:8). By sounding so clearly that prophetic note from the Scriptures, Martin Luther King gave new content to love of country, for the true patriot is the one who works toward the alignment of all persons and groups, all nations, with what God intends—and that breaks beyond the boundaries of any particular nation's dreams of benefits for itself.

The American Dream's Shadow Side

The American dream is indeed many-sided and varied in its most dramatic expressions, some of which are closer to scriptural directions than others. A shadow side stays with the American dream, and this clings so closely because of our culture's tendency to idealize the individual more than the settlement. Huck Finn resolves to "light out for the territory ahead of all the rest, because Aunt Sally wants to civilize him, and that he can't stand!" When we think of civilization as pictures in settlements along the enduring river—buying and selling human beings as slaves, feuding, cheating and being callous toward one another—we sympathize with Huck in his moral and spiritual perspective, his resistance to society.

Huck Finn stands for many other American heroes or heroines, in fiction or real life, who express the ideal of a resourceful, self-reliant, free-standing, forward-thrusting individual who draws upon inner strength while maturing in confrontation with a society that is sometimes kindly but more often hostile, even life-threatening.

Our culture has produced very few stories that portray a "people" being formed, a "people" and not merely a collection of highly differentiated individuals, learning patterns of cooperation more than competition, drawing strength from complementary gifts for the welfare of the total group, delighting in the life enhancement of all, though guarding the dignity and rights of each.

I have in mind a story like that told by Richard Adams in *Watership Down*. Adams writes out of the British rather than the American cultural setting. *Watership Down* is a lively story about rabbits, but really about important elements that contribute to forming a "people," a community. The story reflects some of the same accents in the Scriptures we shall soon highlight. It will help, by way of contrast, to give sharper focus to the American dream's preoccupation with "rugged individualism" if we relate Adam's story in enough detail so that we catch its main story line.

It all begins in the setting of the Sandleford Warren, a comfortable and typical rabbit community, at least in the lively imagination of the author.

Into this warren were born two brothers, Hazel and Fiver. Fiver had special ability to sense danger, which he came to believe was close at hand one day when a sign was posted right in the middle of their grassy meadow. Fiver could not actually read the sign, but he sensed that something dreadful was going to happen. The sign was a notice that their meadow was about to be bulldozed and developed for new office buildings.

Fiver and Hazel tried to warn the chief rabbit and others in the Sandleford Warren. But to no avail.

Finally they decided to leave and were joined by a few other rabbits who believed their message: Bigwig, Blackberry, Dandelion, and Pipkin.

Eventually this pilgrim band of rabbits set out for an unknown country. As they went, they gained in numbers, had adventures, met dangers, made decisions, became a group, faced temptations, and looked for a new home, which Fiver kept forseeing as a place of refuge and great promise.

Hazel emerged as their chief rabbit. It was never clear just how that happened. No one remembered an official vote. Hazel just seemed to have the ability to help the group decide and take the next step at crucial points. He had a kind of authority, even though others around him had more strength, more predictive powers, more ingenuity, more story-telling abilities.

Hazel's Warren left Sandleford, which had become tradition centered and security oriented, and which lacked the spirit of adventure, even the readiness to admit the presence of danger. They still told traditional stories, but largely for comfort and entertainment.

Later in their travels Hazel and his followers met Cowship's Warren, which was freedom centered and featured individual liberties, with each doing what he or she wished. There were almost no stories told to nurture adventure and courage. Hazel and his friends were tempted to settle in Cowslip's Warren, for they liked the freedom. But eventually they moved on. And it was good that they did, for the rabbits in Cowslip's Warren paid a high price for their carefree existence. A farmer was providing them food so he could periodically trap and slaughter them for market.

Still later they met General Woundwort's Warren, which was power centered, organized around centralized authority. When stories were told, they subordinated individual initiative and applauded submission to authority. This too was tempting to Hazel's Warren, but again they continued their quest, having learned some useful things through these encounters.

Finally they arrived at Watership Down, a hilltop, grassy area with peace and abundant food. But Fiver remained restless, still looking toward a future home of even greater promise and beauty.

The rabbits of Hazel's Warren had a spirit of adventure, setting out without knowing where they were going, leaving comfort and security to seek a new home of promise, facing great risks and temptations.

They cared for the weakest among them. Shortly after leaving the Sandleford Warren they came to a river that had to be crossed. Pipkin was too weak to make it. At Blackberry's suggestion they ferried him to the other side on a piece of wood that they found lodged at the river's edge.

They were open to strangers. In their travels they met a mouse and a gull who needed their aid, which they stopped to provide, only to receive great help in return from the mouse and gull as the journey continued.

They made use of different gifts among them: Bigwig's strength, Blackberry's intelligence, Dandelion's storytelling skills, Pipkin's weakness, Fiver's ability to predict the future, and Hazel's authority.

They loved to hear and to tell stories. Not just any stories. Not stories by which they intended to confuse and deceive others. Not

stories that gave them false security and blinded them to the real
temptations and dangers all around them. Not stories that made them
fatalistic and passive in the face of threat and death. Not stories that
made them do unnatural things like fighting so much that they
became very suspicious and no longer able to accept strangers or to
enjoy romping playfully in the dewy fresh grass and the other things
that normally delight rabbits.

The stories they loved reminded them of their earliest beginnings, of their need for each other, for the weakest and the strongest,
even for strangers. It reminded them of the nature of their journey,
filled as it was with promise and trials, hope and adventure. It reminded
them that life itself is a gift to be received with gratitude, trust, and
courage even when the way ahead seemed dark and fearsome.

Watership Down. Quite a different type of story from those
generated within the American culture. It helps illuminate the shadow
side of the fantasy Huck Finn expressed. He constantly desired to
"light out for the territory ahead of all the rest." The price to be paid is
loneliness, a perpetual search for one's home, for belonging, for caring
relationships, at times even accompanied by moodiness, despair,
death. Think of the black despondency that plagued Abe Lincoln, his
anticipation of doom, his yearning for, but scarcely finding, fulfilling
human relationships. Think of Martin Luther King's dream of a new
time of promise, a time when all would be free, and his somber
awareness that, like Moses before him, he could at best see Palestine
from distant Mount Nebo, that the Promised Land was not his to
enter.

Related to this shadow side of the American dream is a constant
yearning and search for community, and so tension persists. I was
reminded of this hunger for human relationships in our culture when a
spiritual retreat was held recently at York Center Church of the
Brethren and Bethany Seminary. Present were members of a ministry
whose calling is to develop a new congregation in Putney, Vermont.
We questioned them about the progress of their ministry in New
England, about where their ministry was leading them. They stated
that hunger for caring relationships was the most evident community
need and focus of their work. New England—Putney, Vermont! The
place of the earliest town meetings, of Yankee ingenuity,
resourcefulness, and independent spirit, yet also reflecting an evident
search for community, for belonging!

The tension in the American dream between preferring heroes
and heroines who are rugged, free-standing individuals while also
yearning for community challenges the church and its faith development and sharing. Because none of us escapes strong cultural formation, we easily miss the Scriptures that speak less of "representative in-

dividuals" and far more of a "representative community." But there are also opportunities for the church to be the church in this setting by embodying in fresh ways the scriptural message about "life in covenant."

If our sight is clear, the Scriptures bring focus to the "church's dream" of "life in a covenant community." They also realistically assess the need for conversion, for a radical change in direction if we are truly to know and enjoy the life in covenant God intends and is working through Christ and the Spirit to achieve.

"Life in covenant" has its foundation in God's promise "I will be your God, and you shall be my people" (Leviticus 26:12).

God covenants to be our God, and God works to form that covenant community into which we are summoned.

On the one hand, there is God's unconditional love and steadfastness in covenant. On the other, there is God's own active engagement in fulfilling the promise of our becoming his people.

There is never any doubt in the Scriptures about whose work it is. It is God's. God is the author of the promise and the active partisan in support of the intended outcome.

Toward this end God works through a particular nation, Israel, and through "anointed servants" whose calling is to help form and strengthen the mission of the "people of the covenant": Abraham and Sarah, Isaac, Jacob, Joseph, Moses and Aaron, Joshua, Samuel, Esther, a succession of judges, Saul, David, Solomon, the kings who followed, Amos, and other prophetic voices.

God worked through a particular person, Jesus of Nazareth

—who insisted that he came not to "abolish the law and the prophets but to fulfill them;"

—and through whom the unexpected breaking out of new life following his crucifixion, the "people of the new covenant, community," or Christ's "resurrection body," are given a new corporate identity.

Life in the new convenant, in the resurrection body, has qualities like those found in a well-functioning orchestra.

Each member of the orchestra has particular gifts and contributions to make.

Each has mastered a specific instrument.

Each has learned to play in harmony with the other members.

And each must follow the conductor, who may even improvise a tune while staying true to the song's basic directions.

As "people of the new covenant," Christ's "resurrection body," we are to follow God's conducting. That requires

—undergoing a radical, continuing conversion;

—being "awakened" out of sleep-like forgetfulness to new obedience;

—experiencing a "falling out" between old patterns and those new responses that befit life in the new covenant! "Whoever is in Christ is a new creature; the old has passed away, behold, the new has come" (2 Corinthians 5:17).

A "falling out" between the "old" and the "new." The "old" persists, as when we presume that we must constantly look out for our own interests, either as individuals or as special interest groupings. *Time* magazine did an essay a while ago on the pervasiveness of group separation and self-protectiveness. The essay's intriguing title was "Local Chauvinism: Long May it Rave." The essay claimed that virtually every community and region in the nation remains convinced that it is distinctive and superior in one respect or another.

Each local region finds something to brag about: Harlan County, Kentucky, its meanness; Arizona, its dry air; Louisiana, its murderous humidity; Texas, it yellow dust; Nashville, its raucous music; Memphis its special quiet since banning auto horns; Apalachicola, Florida, its oysters; Hope, Arkansas, its watermelons.

Each region thrives on disparaging rivals (as one politician after another does in political campaigns). Minneapolis writes off St. Paul as though it were a mill village; Dallas depicts Fort Worth as "the sticks;" South Dakotans believe North Dakotans are an alien race; North Californians regard the state's southern part as a land of incurable kooks.

The old persists in the general culture and in the church. The New Testament church had its continuing struggles, its "falling out," its own estrangements between Gentile and Jews, male and female, slave and free, those gifted with speaking in tongues and those not, the party of Paul and the party of Apollos, those free to eat meat offered to idols and those who found it abhorrent.

Do I need to remind us of our own estrangements and continuing struggles against the presumption we must look out for our personal and group interests? Need I remind us of the forms of group localism, at all levels of church and interchurch life, that become narrow and self-protective, of the barriers we create between ourselves and others?

Nevertheless, the New Testament witness is clear and sure. "The new has come, the old has passed away!" God not only promises, but works powerfully to achieve results. The formation of the new covenant community into which we are summoned is as secure as God's promise that it shall be so. Life in Christ's resurrection body, under Christ's lordship, is as well grounded as Christ's triumph over the powers of darkness.

These New Testament assurances are what may strengthen the

church's faith development and give direction to the church's faith sharing. We continue to live in the tension of our culture between rugged individualism and hunger for caring relationships, in the church's own tension between life in the power of the "new" and residual claims of the "old."

The challenges and the opportunities of the American dream for the church's life and witness will only be met as, by God's grace, we begin to live as those who are not only justified but also sanctified, not only as the recipients of God's forgiving love but as those who in word and deed have been raised to "new life in Christ."

Life in the New Covenant

Grant, O God, that we shall be "awakened" out of the sleep of forgetfulness, that we shall experience a "falling out" between the "old" and the "new" so that we shall faithfully embody and bear witness to life in the covenant, whose foundation is God's own loving purpose set forth in Jesus Christ, the crucified-risen Lord. Amen.